THE INSTITUTIONAL ECONOMICS
OF FOREIGN AID

This book is about the institutions, incentives and constraints, that guide the behaviour of people and organisations involved in the implementation of foreign aid programmes. While traditional performance studies tend to focus almost exclusively on policies and institutions in recipient countries, the book looks at incentives in the entire chain of organisations involved in the delivery of foreign aid, from donor governments and agencies to consultants, experts and other intermediaries. Four aspects of foreign aid delivery are examined in detail: incentives inside donor agencies, the interaction of subcontractors with recipient organisations, incentives inside recipient country institutions, and biases in aid performance monitoring systems.

BERTIN MARTENS is an economist at the European Commission in Brussels. He has worked for various foreign aid organisations, including United Nations agencies and the European Commission, and he is a member of the International Society for New Institutional Economics.

UWE MUMMERT is Professor of Economics at the Georg-Simon-Ohm-University of Applied Sciences in Nuremberg (Germany). His research interests include law and economics and institutional economics, and their application to developing and transition countries. He also works as a consultant in development and transition policy.

PETER MURRELL is Professor of Economics at the University of Maryland and currently holds a Chair on the Academic Council of the Institutional Reform and the Informal Sector (IRIS) Center. He is the author of *The Nature of Socialist Economies* and *Assessing the Value of Law in the Transition to Socialism*, and is a contributor to various journals, including the *American Economic Review* and the *Journal of Comparative Economics*.

PAUL SEABRIGHT is Professor of Economics at the University of Toulouse. His many publications have focused on theoretical and applied microeconomics, and he is currently a Research Fellow at the Centre for Economic Policy Research.

THE INSTITUTIONAL ECONOMICS OF FOREIGN AID

BERTIN MARTENS
UWE MUMMERT
PETER MURRELL
PAUL SEABRIGHT

with a foreword by Elinor Ostrom

CAMBRIDGE
UNIVERSITY PRESS

PUBLISHED BY THE PRESS SYNDICATE OF THE UNIVERSITY OF CAMBRIDGE
The Pitt Building, Trumpington Street, Cambridge, United Kingdom

CAMBRIDGE UNIVERSITY PRESS
The Edinburgh Building, Cambridge CB2 2RU, UK
40 West 20th Street, New York, NY 10011-4211, USA
477 Williamstown Road, Port Melbourne, VIC 3207, Australia
Ruiz de Alarcón 13, 28014 Madrid, Spain
Dock House, The Waterfront, Cape Town 8001, South Africa

http://www.cambridge.org

First published 2002

Printed in the United Kingdom at the University Press, Cambridge

Typeface Baskerville Monotype 11/12.5 pt.   *System* LATEX 2ε [TB]

A catalogue record for this book is available from the British Library

Library of Congress Cataloguing in Publication data
Martens, Bertin.
The institutional economics of foreign aid / Bertin Martens [*et al.*], with
a foreword by Elinor Ostrom.
p.   cm.
Includes bibliographical references and index.
ISBN 0 521 80818 9
1. Economic assistance.   I. Title.
HC60 .M3358   2002   338.91 – dc21   2001043591

ISBN 0 521 80818 9 hardback

Contents

Figures

Foreword

The authors of this excellent book address the question of why international foreign assistance programmes have so rarely achieved the goals set out for them by the donor community. Following the Second World War, despite massive transfers of funds from developed countries to developing countries, many developing countries have seen little improvement in economic growth. The opportunities offered to their populations are still quite limited, even though the record in regard to health statistics has improved more than economic and social conditions in many developing countries. The authors do not attribute the cause to a plot fomented by immoral individuals trying to use public funds for private gain – even though such individuals can be found to operate in this terrain. Rather, the cause is less dramatic, but more plausible. The cause is the set of incentives facing the diverse actors involved in the chain of aid delivery.

All public agencies have been created to achieve multiple goals, but they cannot all be achieved simultaneously. Diverse actors within and outside public agencies are usually more interested in seeing one set of goals accomplished over others. Thus, the public sector is often best characterised as having multiple and sometimes conflicting goals, as well as multiple principals who tend to push for the achievement of different goals.

The four authors of this book – Bertin Martens, Uwe Mummert, Peter Murrell and Paul Seabright – have demonstrated the relevance of the principal–agent model used by contemporary political economists by consistently using it to analyse a diverse set of fascinating questions of central importance to understanding international aid processes. The fundamental problem of all

principal–agent situations is that agents have private information about their own goals and the effort they invest to achieve a
principal's objectives. Consequently, principals have a challenging
task to write a contract to increase the alignment of the interests
of agents with their own interests. In a public agency, the principal
is broadly conceptualised as the general public itself. As the public
cannot be watching its agents on a daily basis, the public must elect
representatives who, in turn, choose implementing agents to carry
out desired public activities. In most public agencies, considerable
slippage occurs along the chain of command from voter to elected
officials to appointed officials to contractor to beneficiaries. Voters,
however, eventually receive most aspects of domestic public services
and can thus broadly assess whether these goods and services are
roughly worth the tax dollars spent on them. This is always a tough
process in a modern democracy where many goods and services
are provided by public agencies, and determining whether tax dollars have been used efficiently is difficult. The voter, however, has
some chance of directly learning how a government jurisdiction is
doing in regard to improving air quality, providing social security,
and policing major highways.

In regard to international assistance, however, the authors point
out that even this weak feedback loop is broken. As Martens states
in his introduction:

a unique and most striking characteristic of foreign aid is that the people
for whose benefit aid agencies work are not the same as those from whom
their revenues are obtained: they actually live in different countries and
different political constituencies. This geographical and political separation between beneficiaries and taxpayers blocks the normal performance
feedback process: beneficiaries may be able to observe performance but
cannot modulate payments (rewards to the agents) in function of performance. (Chapter 1, p. 14)

Many of the problems addressed in the volume are linked closely to
this broken feedback loop.

Several variants of principal–agent models are developed in the
volume. In Chapter 2, 'Conflicts of Objectives and Task Allocation
in Aid Agencies', Paul Seabright develops a multi-task, principal–
agent model that encompasses the idea that agents also have multiple talents. Among the implications from this model are that a

strong decision-making bias exists in this field toward measuring inputs that are easy to monitor rather than outputs that are always more difficult to measure. A second bias is one of ensuring that budgets are spent, rather than that budgets are spent well.

Peter Murrell in Chapter 3, 'The Interaction of Donors, Contractors and Recipients', develops a model of the relations between a donor and a contractor hired to carry the major burden of crafting reforms for a recipient country. As all national reforms are non-excludable and non-subtractive – and thus are public goods – measuring final output is extremely difficult. Some intermediate observable, such as the passage of legislation, is likely to be substituted by the donor as evidence of successful reform. Given that the way a reform operates in practice is affected by how well it fits with a particular socio-economic environment, reform legislation that is based on another country's productive legislation can even be counterproductive when introduced into an entirely different environment. Murrell demonstrates that multiple equilibria are possible, ranging from effective to ineffective reforms depending on how contractual arrangements are negotiated as well as on the configuration of interests.

Continuing with the theme of embedding externally induced institutional reforms in a recipient country, Uwe Mummert models the implementation game after an externally financed *de jure* reform has been accepted by a recipient country. He examines the potential conflict that social norms can create, if induced reforms do not build upon the social structures that have evolved in a recipient country over a long period of time. His good news is that unless extreme social fragmentation exists, rule-violating behaviour is unlikely to become dominant. On the other hand, Mummert stresses that market reforms can never completely lay out all of the do's and don'ts necessary to create a viable, open and competitive market. The problem of direct and indirect conflict between *de jure* and *de facto* institutions is substantially enhanced in fragmented societies where insider–outsider differentiation is deeply rooted.

In his chapter on 'The Role of Evaluations in Foreign Aid Programmes', Bertin Martens points out the major impact of evaluations in a 'democratic' process with a broken feedback loop. Unfortunately, the evaluation process is itself subject to manipulation both by the donor country's development assistance agency as well as by those responsible for aid delivery itself. All too often, under-funded evaluations come so late in the process of aid delivery that the lessons are only relevant for the design of new projects. Aid officials, however, rotate fast enough so that what is learned from one project can rarely be applied by the same official to other projects in the same embedded setting.

Most of the examples in the volume come from multilateral aid processes as major segments of the book were initially formulated in the Evaluation Unit of the European Commission. The lessons, however, are generally relevant for all scholars and long-term aid practitioners interested in improving the performance of interna-tional aid processes. I am sure that others will find as many insightful passages as I did in reading through this useful book.

Elinor Ostrom

1

Introduction

Bertin Martens

This book is about the institutions that guide the behaviour of persons involved in the implementation of foreign aid programmes. Following North (1990), it distinguishes between institutions and organisations. Institutions are the formal and informal rules of behaviour that constitute incentives for all agents involved in the aid delivery process; they affect the performance of foreign aid programmes. Organisations are the groups of persons that adhere to a particular set of these rules. In the case of aid, they include taxpayers and donor organisations, politicians, lobby groups, donor agencies and consultants in donor countries, and recipient organisations in beneficiary countries. This book analyses how these institutions affect the outcomes produced by organisations involved in the aid delivery process. It diverges from more traditional approaches to aid performance because it seeks to explain that performance in terms of incentives inside the aid delivery process, rather than recipient country policy performance. The proposed approach also differs from game-theoretic models that attempt to explain aid performance in terms of outcomes of strategic interactions between donors and recipients at macro-institutional level. This book goes down to micro-level decision-making processes and behaviour by agents working in donor agencies, subcontractors hired by these agencies and officials working in beneficiary country organisations. It will show that incentives and constraints for individual agents can diverge significantly from those of the organisation that they work for and thus lead to very different behavioural outcomes from those predicted by macro-institutional approaches. On the other hand, the models and analysis presented in this book are sufficiently general to be applicable not only to conditionality-based institutional and policy reform programmes but also to non-conditional aid and more traditional investment projects.

It is also a book about the use of foreign aid to achieve institutional and policy reform in recipient countries. In our view, the performance of donor-induced reform programmes is correlated with the institutional set-up of donor agencies and aid programmes to deliver these reforms. Donors cannot realistically and successfully tackle institutional reform questions in recipient countries if they do not have an appropriate institutional set-up in place to deliver the required types of aid in a credible manner. For instance, a project-based approach to institutional reforms may be more exposed to moral hazard problems than a conditionality-based approach; project approaches allocate aid to inputs while conditionality approaches pay for results. Alternatively, recipient countries cannot expect to receive appropriate technical and political support for their reform plans from donors that do not have the institutional technology to deliver their contributions in a credible way. This book examines how the switch from traditional investment projects to institutional reform programmes affects performance incentives for individual agents involved in aid implementation as well as the overall performance of a donor agency.

The idea to research the subject of this book originally arose in the foreign aid Evaluation Unit of the European Commission (EC). In the summer of 1997, I was working with a few colleagues and consultants on two global performance reports of EC-financed Phare and Tacis institutional reform programmes in the transition economies of Central and Eastern Europe. We had worked our way through a pile of monitoring and evaluation reports on individual Phare and Tacis projects, interviewed many programme managers and consultants and completed some fieldwork as well. While we were compiling a synthesis report, we were struck by the convergence of views that emerged out of this apparently chaotic pile of information. There were many similarities in project design, implementation and outcomes, in behaviour of project managers and policy decisions, despite a wide diversity of project circumstances, across countries, sectors and types of projects. Evaluation reports on EC programmes in other regions of the world revealed similar patterns. Surely, there had to be common factors and incentives in the EC aid delivery process that generated these similarities in outcomes, out of a diversity of situations.

To illustrate this point, let me just cite a few of these general findings. A Phare evaluation report (European Commission, 1997, pp.55–56) concluded that there is 'a tendency for the Commission to contract out expertise in the transition process and retain in-house expertise in financial and administrative procedures... strong emphasis on financial and procedural control rather than substantive design and performance' and contracts were 'based on inputs and activities specifications rather than on outputs and effective results'. An evaluation report on the EC's Mediterranean aid (European Commission, 1998) concluded that multiple objectives came without 'a comprehensive analysis of the linkages and interconnections between different policy objectives' and consequently 'no goal hierarchy, leaving the Commission with unclear guidance for aid management and implementation'. The frequent recurrence of these and similar findings indicated that aid programme performance was not only determined by the particular circumstances of individual project managers and recipient countries but also – and perhaps predominantly – by the incentives embedded in the institutional environment of the aid agency and its aid delivery process. These findings may not sound terribly original to persons who have had any substantial involvement in aid delivery. However, the virtual absence of any studies of incentive structures in aid delivery processes is even more striking. This book is an attempt to fill that gap.

This shift of attention from recipient country performance to incentive mechanisms in the aid delivery process is not entirely new. To some extent, a number of macro-level aid performance studies published during the 1990s already paved the way. These studies aimed to find a correspondence between changes in aid volumes and changes in macro-economic variables in the beneficiary countries (White, 1992; Boone, 1994; Tsikata, 1998). Generally, they conclude that foreign aid has no tangible impact on economic growth in the recipient countries. Burnside and Dollar's (1996, 2000) landmark study came to similar conclusions. However, the authors qualified this finding with the remark that aid does indeed have a positive impact on growth when the policy environment in the recipient country is conducive to growth. It also raised the question of the direction of causality: does aid cause good policies, or do good policies induce aid flows? In other words, does aid have an active or a passive role to play in policy and institutional reforms in beneficiary countries?

Dollar and Svensson (1998) are cautious about the direction of causality. An analysis of a sample of World Bank policy-based loans revealed that donor efforts have no significant impact on recipient country policy performance. Policy outcomes are basically generated by domestic political environments, not by donor influence. This suggests a more passive role for donor agencies: selecting genuine reformers and using aid programmes as a commitment device to ensure that the reformers are not derailed from their mission. It puts responsibility for the success (or failure) of aid programmes more squarely on the shoulders of the recipients.

However, Dollar and Svensson (1998) also note that about one-third of all World Bank structural adjustment loans fail to meet their policy targets but are nevertheless paid out in most cases. This happens because the Bank does not only care altruistically about economic development but also more egoistically about a country's ability to service previous Bank loans. Furthermore, other donors and creditors may pressure the Bank to provide financial resources that enable a country to continue servicing its debt. If this happens regularly, borrowers will not fail to notice the creditor's lack of commitment to his own commitment devices. Clearly, moral hazard can occur on the donor side too. This demonstrates that the donor's policy stance and own internal incentives do indeed matter for the outcome of aid programmes and would lead to a more balanced conclusion whereby donors and recipients share responsibility for the success or failure of aid programmes.

Over the years, the debate on the respective roles and responsibilities of donor agencies and recipient governments has moved away from desired policy and institutional reform outcomes to the processes of reform, including how incentives and constraints influence outcomes. When an optimal outcome is not achieved, it is usually not because of lack of knowledge about this outcome among decision-makers but rather because optimising agents face incentives and constraints that deviate their behaviour from this target (Ranis and Mahmood, 1992). More than a decade after the start of the great economic transition wave in former communist countries, donor agencies have apparently not digested this message. They continue to blame poor reform performance on obnoxious recipients, rather than examine the weaknesses in incentives inside donor and recipient institutions.

There is a substantial volume of political science and political economy literature that discusses political processes and the factors that affect policy and institutional reform outcomes in developing countries, with or without the intervention of foreign aid agencies (Haggard and Webb, 1994; Devarajan *et al.*, 1999). There is also a substantial volume of game-theoretic research on the interplay between aid donors and beneficiaries and devices to reduce the probabilities of moral hazard in this relationship (Collier *et al.*, 1997; Mosley, 1997; Svensson, 1997). That is the nearest that the literature gets to examining the impact of incentives inside the aid delivery process itself on aid outcomes.

This book intends to dig deeper inside the organisations involved in aid delivery and the institutional incentives that are at work in these organisations. It looks at the role of development organisations in the effectiveness of foreign aid and concentrates on intermediary processes, in between the macro-level at which the first allocation decisions are made and the local scene where outcomes become visible.

The aid literature on these subjects is very scarce. A study by Quarles *et al.* (1988) is an exceptional early forerunner in this approach. It is one of the first to take a critical look at institutional incentives and organisational arrangements inside aid delivery processes. Their explanation for the rationale of their research fits very well into the purposes of the present book and deserves a full citation:

[Aid] agencies are not just rational, neutral tools of policy makers and as such external to the problems of development . . . Special attention is given to the linkages or relationships between development agencies at different levels of organization. Each one is part of increasingly long and complex chains of interdependent organizations. The other units constitute a vital part of its environment. These linkages, therefore, are a major concern in the contributions. In a sense, all development organizations are intermediate bodies, part of a wider network through which the money flows. (Quarles *et al.*, 1988, p.12)

The quality of aid is directly related to the ways in which it is organized. To what extent are the agencies capable of producing the results they aim at? What are their capabilities and constraints? (Quarles *et al.*, 1988, p.11)

Carr *et al.* (1998, p.44) offer a similar perspective on aid delivery. Their analysis of the effectiveness of aid is based on the idea that:

... at each link in the [aid delivery] chain, there exists an agenda which may or may not be consistent with the agendas both below and above it. These inconsistent and often conflicting agendas in the aid chain create difficulties in the determination of expected outcomes for any particular project.

Recently, a study launched by the Swedish International Development Agency (SIDA) has also examined incentive issues in the interactions between the agents and organisations involved in the delivery of foreign aid, based on more empirical observation of aid delivery processes (Ostrom *et al.*, 2001).

2. INSTITUTIONAL ECONOMICS AND AGENCY THEORY

This book applies a particular type of institutional analysis, usually labelled as 'agency theory', to analyse the incentive problems that may occur in foreign aid delivery. This section explains why we have chosen to follow that path, situates it in modern institutional economics, and shows how it applies to the institutions of foreign aid.

As this book is about institutions, it naturally applies the techniques and insights of institutional economics. Modern institutional economics is a tree with many branches and twigs. The terminology 'institutional economics' covers a wide range of schools of thought and methods. It includes several varieties of transaction costs economics, from Coase (1937, 1960) to Williamson (1985) and North (1990), as well as various branches of organisation theory, including property rights (Grossman and Hart, 1986), incomplete contracts theory (Tirole, 1999), and its analysis of organisational design (Holmstrom and Milgrom, 1991; Aghion and Tirole, 1997). This is not the place to explain the details of each of these schools. Interested readers are referred to more general handbooks of institutional and organisational economics (Laffont and Tirole, 1993; Furubotn and Richter, 1998; Masten and Williamson, 1999).

All these schools of institutional economic thought have a common characteristic: they examine how informational problems affect organisational performance, though from different angles. That is precisely what distinguishes neo-classical from neo-institutional economics. While the former generally assumes that (near-)perfect information is available in transactions at (near-)zero costs, the latter assumes positive information costs. Transaction cost economics looks at the cost of obtaining information required to conclude a contract or exchange (North, 1990) and the potential costs of post-contractual uncertainty or absence of information (Williamson, 1985). Incomplete contracts theory is based on quite similar principles but focuses on the incentives embedded in a contract and the likely behavioural outcomes that they produce under imperfect information (Tirole, 1999). Property rights theory examines how different allocations of this residual contractual uncertainty create different incentive structures. Modern organisation theory combines these different techniques to study incentives and delegation of tasks in large organisations or hierarchies. Institutions – rules of behaviour – exist precisely because they are means to partially overcome these informational problems and the resulting uncertainties. Bilateral contracts, general laws and informal agreements ensure that some of these are kept within acceptable limits. However, they cannot create a risk-free world and we have to live with these residual uncertainties in our daily activities, including in the delivery of foreign aid.

This book applies these insights to informational problems that may occur in the various steps of the delivery process of foreign aid from the donor to the final beneficiary. It examines how these informational problems induce biases in the behaviour of agents involved in this process and how this affects the ultimate performance of aid programmes. Fortunately, it also attempts to explain how some of these problems can be tackled through clever institutional design.

The four studies in this book use a common methodological approach and apply the techniques of only one branch of modern neo-institutional economics, namely principal–agent or agency theory. Principal–agent theory starts from the simple observation that modern organisations are usually hierarchically structured, with principals giving instructions to agents. Principals in a company, a club or a public administration, cannot take all decisions and carry out all tasks themselves. They need to delegate at least part of the work to agents. While the principal appropriates the benefits (and costs) of the task, the agent receives a reward – a wage, a stock option, a promotion, etc. – in return for carrying out the specified tasks. Delegation implies that the principal does not have full information about the activities of the agent. If principals want to have full information and to monitor every aspect of agents' activities, then they might as well carry out the delegated tasks themselves; there would be no gain from delegation. Delegation may result in two types of problems. Firstly, agents may deviate from the instructions given by the principal and carry out delegated tasks in such a way that they advance their own interests, rather than those of the principal. This is called moral hazard. Secondly, at the time of reaching agreement with the principal, the agent may have access to information inaccessible to the principal, and may manipulate this information in ways that run against the principal's interests (as when sellers of second-hand cars are more likely to offer low-quality cars for sale, or when counterfeit money drives out good, as classically described in Gresham's Law). This is called adverse selection. Both problems lower the return from the task for the principal, compared to the return under perfect information.

Moral hazard and adverse selection are unavoidable consequences of delegation of tasks in organisations. Large-scale organisations, like aid agencies, usually consist of multiple layers of delegation. Consequently, a wide variety of incentive problems can occur at different levels of delegation and should be addressed through appropriate institutional design. The art of good design consists of mitigating these problems by setting up incentive structures that motivate agents to reveal relevant information to the principal and reduce biases in their behaviour.

Agency theory has found a wide range of applications to virtually every aspect of organisation and contracts (Laffont and Tirole, 1993). It is therefore somewhat surprising to see that there are, as yet, very few traces of applications in the development economics and foreign aid literature to the organisations involved in the implementation of foreign aid.

A major exception to this statement is the use of principal–agent models in the study of conditionality contracts between donors and recipients of aid (Pietrobelli and Scarpa, 1990; Trombetta, 1992; Killick, 1995). Murshed and Sen (1995) use a principal–agent model to capture the stylised facts of multilateral aid negotiations on non-economic conditionality such as military expenditure reduction. Collier *et al.* (1997) discuss conditionality problems in aid but their analysis is only implicitly based on an agency approach. Rodrik (1997) examines the advantages of multilateral donor agencies in imposing effective conditionality. In fact, the entire conditionality debate is about principal–agent relations: a donor requests a recipient to do something, in return for receiving aid. Recipient compliance with the agreement is subject to moral hazard and adverse selection. Streeten (1988) reformulated the principal–agent problem in aid conditionality very pointedly: 'Why would a donor pay a recipient to do something that is anyway in his own interest? And if it is not in his interest, why would the recipient do it anyway?' As explained above, applications of agency models to conditionality are generally situated at a macro-institutional level, exploring the outcomes of direct negotiations between a donor agency and a recipient government. They do not examine differences in incentive structures and agents' behaviour within the donor or recipient organisation as a result of delegation of tasks – which is precisely the subject of the present book. In a way, the conditionality issue could be considered as a special case of a more general agency problem, namely when both the donor and the recipient organisation acts as a single homogenous agent.

Frey *et al.* (1985) are more explicit about the difference between the macro-and micro-institutional approach and suggest that there are two ways to model the behaviour of (international) organisations. Either the organisation is treated as an aggregate unit possessing well-defined preferences or the different interests of individual members of the organisation are considered and the behaviour of the organisation as a whole is taken to be the outcome of the individuals' actions. Frey *et al.* chose the first option for their model of World Bank lending behaviour, partly because the availability of organisation-level data sets allowed them to test the organisation's behavioural assumptions. This book has chosen the second option, because our analysis of foreign aid organisations has led to the conclusion that there is indeed strong divergence of interests between the various agents involved in aid delivery, even though they may contractually be committed to the same organisation and aid programme objectives.

The main disadvantage of our methodological option is the lack of empirical data sets to test the models. Aid agencies, non-governmental organisations (NGOs), aid services suppliers or other organisations involved in foreign aid do not normally collect intra-organisational data on the behaviour of individual employees, their motivation, incentives and effort spent on different tasks, or their objectives and strategic behaviour in negotiations with agents of other organisations. Collecting such data would require surveys, personal interviews, detailed analysis of resource allocations and procedural complexity in aid organisations, etc. It is not the purpose of this book to empirically test the models and assumptions presented. Some of these are illustrated with *ad hoc* examples only. This book is meant to lay the more theoretical foundations for empirical approaches to the institutional economics of foreign aid. As such, it provides a basis for an empirical research agenda that will require considerable data collection efforts.

This research project was not just an attempt to find new applications of agency theory. It is used as an analytical tool to generate novel findings about the performance of aid organisations, institutions and implementation processes that go beyond existing development aid research, including research on aid conditionality. Before we look at the findings of the individual studies in this book we first scrutinise – in the next section – the existing principal–agent literature and examine to what extent some of its major findings can be transplanted to the institutions and organisations of foreign aid and yield novel insights concerning their performance.

3. SOME BASIC CHARACTERISTICS OF FOREIGN AID ORGANISATIONS

Foreign aid grants are usually paid by citizens in a donor country, either as taxes channelled through an official aid agency or as voluntary donations given to NGOs. Aid is not normally collected and dispensed by private for-profit enterprises, unless they have set up a separate charitable organisation. However, private agents and enterprises may act as subcontractors in the execution of aid projects. Alternatively, foreign aid loans channelled through development banks are mobilised on international financial markets and passed on to recipient countries. Both loans and grants can be handled through bilateral as well as multilateral aid agencies. Both official and non-governmental agencies share some of the typical characteristics of public administrations.

Multiple principals and objectives

Economic analysis of public administrations started with Simon (1958) and Downs (1967). However, agency theory and asymmetric information models to investigate the behaviour of organisations did not emerge until the 1970s. Most applications focused on private organisations where contractual exchange plays an important role. Applications to public administrations emerged only fairly recently (Holmstrom and Milgrom, 1991; Martimort, 1991; Tirole, 1994). The informational characteristics that distinguish public administrations from private enterprises can be summarised as follows:

(a) While private enterprises have only one objective – profit – public administrations usually have multiple objectives. An official bilateral aid agency aims, for instance, to build schools, hospitals, roads and to finance small-scale enterprises and privatisation programmes.

(b) While private enterprises have multiple principals (shareholders) who share the same objective – profit – public administrations have multiple principals (politicians, parliamentarians, etc.) who rarely share objectives.[1] While parliamentarians with construction companies in their constituencies may prefer to allocate more resources to road construction in developing countries, others, with medical research laboratories in theirs, may want to prioritise research into AIDS prevention.

(c) While private companies can measure the opportunity cost of alternative options in terms of profits, public administrations have no clearly defined or measurable trade-off between their multiple options. This is likely to result in potential inconsistencies and contradictions, and inefficient resource allocation. Political principals (parliamentarians) may delegate an unclear or even inconsistent set of instructions to an official aid agency; consequently, the agency cannot perform optimally.

The organisational characteristics of NGOs are not fundamentally different from those of official aid agencies. They have multiple principals (members) who may share a vaguely defined objective ('combat poverty') but hold a variety of opinions on the more detailed objectives (give food aid, provide education, support enterprises) and the trade-offs between these often hard-to-verify objectives. Still, as membership is voluntary and NGOs tend to rally around specific issues or normative stances, they tend to have rather convergent preferences among their members. At the extreme end of the spectrum, single-issue NGOs have an advantage in this respect: their field of action is narrowly defined and resources will be more concentrated. On the other hand, they may be more dependent on internal grass-roots democracy procedures and reaching a concensus, which increases internal transaction costs to arrive at a decision. Because of the problem of multiple principals and objectives, both official aid organisations and NGOs require general policy 'slogans' behind which all members can rally and that hide differences of opinion on objectives and trade-offs: 'fight against poverty', 'first things first', 'aid, not trade', etc. However, semantic synthesis is usually not enough to overcome the potential for inconsistencies in the underlying objectives.

---

[1] In agency theory, multiple principals situations are known as joint delegation of tasks.

These informational characteristics complicate the internal organisation of public administrations in general and official aid agencies in particular, and NGOs. They affect organisational performance and the incentives for individual agents in organisations to pursue their tasks.

Performance incentives are necessarily weak in public administrations (Dixit, 1997). Civil servants usually have a fixed salary and, from time to time, a promotion to a higher salary level. Performance-linked salaries, based on a single measurable and consistent indicator, would be hard to define in most public services. Even if it would be feasible, it would create trouble because it would steer officials towards a single goal, thereby neglecting some of the others goals and disrupting any political consensus among multiple political principals on their multiple objectives. This is an intrinsic predicament of public administrations. In official aid agencies, pay is usually fixed and not linked to any performance indicator. Some multilateral development banks (MDBs) link pay to the volume of loans approved. This could result in biased performance incentives, steering loan officers away from wider development objectives and undermining the financial viability of the bank.

Another consequence of multiple principals and objectives is procedural bias in public administrations, including in aid agencies. McCubbins *et al.* (1988) explain how elected political principals impose administrative procedures on their unelected implementation agents that reduce discretionary decision-making margins. This keeps ownership of decisions in the hands of the politicians. At the same time, bureaucracies have a tendency to develop their own procedures and increase their complexity beyond those imposed on them by their political principals. Bureaucrats do this because risk-taking is not rewarded in a fixed salary system. There is no incentive to appropriate the consequences of risky decisions. Elaborate and complex procedures help to avoid exposure and diffuse risks, especially in those domains where political pressure is highest. For instance, bilateral agencies will establish elaborate consultation networks and procedures with NGOs in their own country, less so with NGOs in recipient countries. They will work out complex tender and contract procedures to diffuse possible criticism from aid services suppliers, but they will allocate comparatively less resources to the verification of the ultimate results of aid projects.

Multilateral aid agencies may be somewhat shielded against direct political pressure from their member states. Firstly, to the extent that they are banks and dispense foreign aid in the form of loans, they do not spend tax revenue. This reduces political pressures associated with spending decisions on tax money. Secondly, although development banks do not pursue profit targets *per se*, they need to ensure their financial viability. This puts constraints on the range of development aid options and objectives that they can pursue. Thirdly, even if they do operate on the basis of grants financed from tax revenue, they can often play-off member states with different objectives against each other and build majority coalitions in the Board to advance the agency's interests. In the case of the United Nations Development Programme (UNDP), where both donors and beneficiaries are members of the decision-making council, this often results in a stand-off between net contributors and net recipients with the latter representing a majority in terms of countries. In the case of the EC, only donor countries are members of the decision-making council. However, the unanimity rule in European Union (EU), decision-making makes it harder for the EC to play off member states against each other.

A broken information feedback loop

The above cases of multiple principals and objectives have been analysed in detail in the relevant agency theory literature and are easily applicable to various types of aid agencies. However, a unique and most striking characteristic of foreign aid is that the people for whose benefit aid agencies work are not the same as those from whom their revenues are obtained; they actually live in different countries and different political constituencies. This geographical and political separation between beneficiaries and taxpayers blocks the normal performance feedback process: beneficiaries may be able to observe performance but cannot modulate payments (rewards to the agents) as a function of performance. Although donors are typically interested in ensuring that their funds are well spent, it is extremely difficult for them to do so, since there is frequently no obvious mechanism for transmitting the beneficiaries' view to the sponsors. Even if such a mechanism existed, beneficiaries' views are likely to be biased because, firstly, they do not pay for their benefits and, secondly, their preferences and objectives are unlikely to fully coincide with those of the donors. In addition, ascertaining the beneficiaries' views in developing countries – often with low levels of democracy and literacy – may not be easy, or even possible, in many cases. Instead, the sponsors must rely on various indirect indicators of programme performance.

This typical characteristic of foreign aid delivery processes stands at odds with the established neo-classical view of the efficiency of public institutions, as originally formulated by Becker (1983) and recently restated by Whitman (1995). According to that view, competition between politicians to get (re-)elected makes them exercise pressure on public institutions to do what the beneficiaries – whom they represent – want. Dissatisfied taxpayers and beneficiaries can lean on their political representatives to exercise political pressure on the public administration or agency to improve the performance of particular transfer programmes. The efficiency hypothesis assumes that donors and beneficiaries are well-informed about the programmes. In the case of foreign aid, geographical and political separation between these two groups increases the costs and decreases the benefits of information. For taxpayers and donors, it is very costly to obtain reliable information on the outcomes of the programmes that they finance. The intended beneficiaries are not voters in the country that pays for the aid and thus have no real political leverage over domestic politicians who approve these programmes, which allows the latter to use these programmes for different political purposes.

This broken feedback loop induces stronger incentive biases in foreign aid – compared to domestic wealth transfer programmes – diverting it from its original purposes. It explains, for instance, why the interests of domestic suppliers of aid goods and services – consultancy companies, experts, suppliers of goods – dominate decision making: they are the direct beneficiaries of aid (they receive the contractually agreed reward) and have direct leverage on domestic political decision-makers. They have first-hand information on the outcomes of the aid programmes in beneficiary countries and they are part of the constituency of the decision-makers in the donor country. Their informational advantage may make them the ultimate beneficiaries of foreign aid. By contrast, the intended beneficiaries' interests are geographically and politically too remote to overcome the direct beneficiaries' leverage. This shift away from a neo-classical perfect information feedback loop to a broken information feedback loop typical in foreign aid is probably one of the most important contributions of this book to the debate on the performance of foreign aid.

The institutional reform dimension

Apart from the above-described inherent problems of foreign aid, including multiple principals and objectives and a broken information feedback loop, there is a third institutional and informational dimension that runs through the studies in this book: the increasing focus of foreign aid programmes on institutional reforms in the recipient countries.

This shift in the composition of foreign aid started in the 1980s, when foreign aid programmes shifted away from a pure investment project focus towards policy and institutional reform. This shift occurred because of a growing awareness that recipient countries lacked an appropriate institutional and policy environment to make aid work in a competitive market environment and because of donor and creditor concerns about the deteriorating financial situation of many developing countries in the early 1980s. To meet these concerns, a fast-disbursing non-project financial instrument was required in the form of structural adjustment programmes that targeted financial aid on overall balance of payments and budgetary support, not on specific investment projects. Disbursement was usually conditional on economic policy changes and institutional reforms. It accelerated in the early 1990s when the so-called transition economies emerged on the foreign aid scene. The wave of transitions from centrally planned to market economies further emphasised the need for institutional and policy reform programmes.[2]

---

[2] 'Institutional reform' and 'policy reform' are considered as virtually synonymous expressions in this text: all government economic policies, and changes therein, aim to redistribute wealth, either directly through fiscal redistribution or indirectly through changes in property rights systems. All these policies are implemented through changes in formal institutions or legal systems.

In the case of EU foreign aid, for instance, the shift towards institutional reform is quite obvious. In the early 1990s, the Phare and Tacis technical assistance programmes for the transition economies in Eastern Europe emerged. They focused predominantly on institutional reform. By 1999, they represented nearly one-third of all EC-managed foreign aid (European Commission, 2000). In the meantime, EC aid to sub-Saharan Africa, the Mediterranean, Asia and Latin America also shifted attention to institution building. Last but not least, the growing volume of institutional economics studies of development issues has no doubt served as a more theoretical platform in support of this trend. Many studies have demonstrated the strong positive correlation between the quality of institutions and the level of economic development (World Bank, 1997; Clague, 1998).

This shift away from traditional investment projects towards institutional reform programmes has implications in terms of performance incentives in principal–agent relations in foreign aid implementation, as well as for the overall performance of foreign aid programmes. Traditional investment projects produce tangible outputs that are fairly easily verifiable and measurable, such as roads, schools and hospitals, institutional reform programmes produce less tangible outputs that are much harder to verify. Reform projects produce intangible outputs, such as draft laws, organisational reform plans, policy advice and trained staff. Their ultimate impact is more diffuse and hard to verify and consequently more easily subject to post-contractual uncertainties. To the extent that aid aims to achieve institutional reforms in the recipient country, monitoring of outcomes and impact becomes more difficult compared to traditional investment projects. Increased difficulty and cost of monitoring facilitates moral hazard and adverse selection in foreign aid programmes, and makes it easier to diverge programmes from their original purposes.

4. PERFORMANCE INCENTIVES IN THE FOREIGN AID DELIVERY CHAIN

Let us now move from these general institutional and informational aspects of foreign aid to the more specific findings of the studies in this book. Each study focuses on a different set of institutions and agents in the aid delivery process and examines their specific informational problems. In a standard official bilateral aid setting, the chain of principal agent relationships starts with taxpayers as principals, who wish to transfer part of their income to recipients in other countries. They delegate the implementation of this transfer programme to their representatives (parliamentarians, politicians) who become their agents. These agents, in turn, become the political principals to an aid agency in charge of implementation of aid programmes. Within the aid agency, a hierarchical command chain creates a further series of principal–agent relationships. When actual implementation is subcontracted to a private consultant or aid services supplier company, the task manager in the aid agency becomes a principal to the contractor; the latter becomes an agent to the task manager. Depending on the contract, the contractor may also be an agent to the recipient agency or counterpart administrator in the beneficiary country. The contractor may end up being an agent to two principals – a typical joint delegation situation. The recipient agent, in turn, is an agent to political principals and the beneficiary population in the recipient country. Each of these principal–agent interfaces in the long chain of command creates a potential for incentive misalignment and moral hazard. As such, the final outcome of the aid process may be quite different from the original objective envisaged by the taxpayer, the aid agency or the recipients.

Many variations on this standard chain of command are possible. Aid agencies may choose to implement a project directly, without passing through a private contractor; or they may provide non-project structural adjustment aid that does not require implementation through technical assistance. Alternatively, donor country citizens may prefer to allocate aid through an NGO. This skips the political representation part of the scheme but decision-making needs to be done anyway, by the (Board) members of the NGO. Another alternative is to channel aid through multilateral grant-in-aid organisations, such as the UNDP or the EC. In that case, several donor country governments delegate implementation responsibility to a multilateral organisation; again a case of joint delegation. Last but not least, donor country governments may set up a multilateral development bank that mobilises financial resources on international capital markets rather than using taxpayers' money.

Each of the four papers in this book looks at a specific part of the principal–agent chain. Paul Seabright examines performance incentives inside donor agencies. Peter Murrell analyses the incentives in the interactions between donors, contractors and recipients. Uwe Mummert investigates what happens inside the recipient country once the recipient government has decided to formally adopt a donor's institutional reform proposal. My own study covers the evaluation feedback loop between the contractor's performance and the donor's aid objectives. The studies emphasise institutional and policy reform programmes and not more traditional investment projects, though many of their findings may be applicable to the latter type of aid as well. The main difference between institutional reform and investment projects is that the outputs of the latter type are mostly physical and therefore more readily observable and measurable, making them less easily subject to moral hazard and adverse selection. The trend towards more institutional reform aid thus increases the probability of moral hazard in aid.

Performance incentives inside aid agencies

Chapter 2, by Paul Seabright, examines the incentives and biases in the behaviour of foreign aid agencies. He focuses on two informational problems in aid agency behaviour, namely inputs bias as a result of the broken feedback loop and problems caused by multiple principals and objectives.

Typically, officials in an aid agency perform a multiplicity of tasks – which is quite normal for large organisations. However, depending on their incentives, certain tasks will receive more attention than others. The disruption in the performance–payment feedback loop, combined with the difficulties of measuring performance, results in an apparently disproportionate focus on 'input' activities – budgets, personnel – at the expense of attention given to the quality of 'outputs' – the actual results of the aid programme. Budgets, contracts and spending on projects are relatively easy to monitor compared to the outputs produced by the projects or the impact of these outputs, especially when institutional reform projects are concerned. The interdependence of tasks means that incentives for the performance of one will affect the performance of the other, either positively or negatively. For instance, one task may be the preparation of project proposals while the other consists of screening them in a quality support group: the more rigorous the screening, the fewer proposals will pass. Another example concerns positive complementarity between financial management and project implementation: the more efficient the former, the smoother the latter.

Two ideas are important here. Firstly, when agents' salaries are not directly linked to ostensible performance, demonstration of their abilities and career concerns dominate their behaviour. Secondly, when agents face multiple tasks that compete for their time, they will focus on those that are more likely to satisfy their career concerns. This may motivate them to focus on tasks that are more easily monitorable by their superiors. However, to the extent that easily (e.g. input-related) and less easily (e.g. output- or results-related) monitorable tasks are complementary and equally important for the overall performance of aid programmes, management will have to ensure that incentives for easily monitored tasks are less high-powered in order to avoid agents diverting effort away from less easily monitored but still important tasks. Reality is often different however. Careers are often built on demonstrating good performance in more easily monitorable tasks, such as 'committing and spending budgets'. This may provide an explanation for the 'inputs bias' that is so often observed in aid agency behaviour (European Commission, 1997).

On the other hand, organisations may rationally place 'too much' emphasis on input tasks, provided these reveal information about talents that may be valuable in output tasks, and in spite of the fact that the incentives to perform the output tasks well will thereby be blunted. Separating the input tasks from the output tasks would be too costly in terms of failing to exploit the links between these skills. Bundling the tasks together may be the lesser of two evils even though it inevitably leads to a misallocation of agents' efforts towards the inputs. Separation of tasks is important for relatively junior members of an agency, because of the greater information about their skills that such separation yields. Too much generalism among junior staff makes it harder to allocate them subsequently to responsible positions in the organisation. Empirical studies of bureaucracy have often failed to distinguish between those aspects of bureaucratic behaviour that reflect poor organisational design and those that are unavoidable consequences of the kind of activity the organisation is obliged to undertake. Some features of organisations, though perhaps regrettable, are the inevitable result of the fact that individuals' behaviour cannot be precisely monitored.

Multilateral aid agencies, like the World Bank or the EC, are cases of joint delegation from multiple principals or member states. On the one hand, joint delegation may induce credible competition between members, enhance the credibility of the agency and allow it to resist pressure from individual members. For instance, it may enable the agency to commit itself to procedures that would not be easy to implement for a bilateral donor, such as transparent and competitive procedures for tendering and procurement, and a commitment to avoid linking aid to narrow considerations of market access or the fortunes of particular political and economic interest groups. However, this commitment may be easier to deliver on the side of input procedures (tendering and contracting) than on the side of the preparation and selection of projects. This latter fact further reinforces the input bias already described. Joint delegation may also achieve economies of scale and scope. For instance, a single aid accounting system or a single set of procedures can be shared by different aid instruments. Multilateralism can also enable the exploitation of economies of scale and scope that are beyond the capacity of bilateral donors.

Joint delegation may on the other hand result in confusion over objectives, or in agencies pursuing their own interests. For instance, sharing of tasks may generate distortionary incentives and divided loyalties to different principals. Another example is that of a multilateral aid agency that reports on the 'needs' of beneficiary countries and may have an incentive to exaggerate these needs in order to boost the importance of the agency. Similarly, it may bias reporting on the beneficial impact of aid programmes to justify its activities. Other beneficiary countries and member states may be aware of this over-reporting but not take any action because it benefits them too when their turn comes. The potential for wide variations in performance in cases of joint delegation indicates that a multilateral agency that fails to exploit the benefits that come from the presence of multiple principals is actually likely to perform worse than bilateral donors. If it cannot find ways to exploit the benefits of multiple principals, then it cannot really justify its existence.

Moral hazard in donor–contractor–recipient relations

Chapter 3, by Peter Murrell, moves away from donor agencies and into the domain of interactions between donors, their (sub) contractors and the recipients of the aid. He also focuses more on the specific incentive problems posed by institutional reform aid and identifies the following actors in a principal–agent model: the donor principal (the political superiors in donor agencies), the donor agent (the direct administrator of a programme, a task manager), the contractor (a profit-seeking consultancy or a non-profit NGO) who has a contractual relationship with the donor agent, the recipient principal (political superiors in the recipient agency), the recipient agent (the institution that is the formal beneficiary of the project). Given the inherently incomplete contract between donor agent and contractor, there is a margin for manoeuvre in project implementation. The equilibrium outcome will depend on who is in control, the contractor, the recipient, or both. Each of these situations is likely to push the actual project outcome away from the intended outcome. The model allows us to examine two sources of information problems that are at the basis of this performance bias.

The first issue is moral hazard in the donor–contractor–recipient relationship – caused by incomplete contract and imperfect knowledge about the contractor's activities, especially in the implementation of institutional reform programmes. As explained earlier, the latter produce less tangible outputs, which leaves more freedom to the contractor, whose reward is not dependent on achievement of targets but who usually receives a fixed lump sum payment only. As a result, the contractor may collide with the recipient to bend the project to their common interest. Traditional inputs-driven project-based approaches to institutional reform, as practised by most technical assistance programmes, such as the EC's Phare and Tacis programmes, are therefore unlikely to yield the intended results. The nature of the contractor, whether a non-profit NGO or a profit-seeking consultancy, affects project implementation. Non-profit contractors may be inclined to forgo contractual rents in order to achieve a reform agenda; for-profit contractors are not. It may thus be better to contract implementation of institutional reforms to NGOs that specialise in the issue at hand. This suggests that important project implementation decisions will be in the hands of the implementers, those working on the ground. These decisions cannot be contracted, because of imperfect information. They also cannot be second-guessed during evaluation, or at least during any evaluation that is not based on knowledge as intimate as that of the implementers.

This brings us to the second issue that goes to the core of the institutional reform debate: the desirable extent of foreign donor leverage in domestic reforms and the representativeness of the recipient organisation. In the 'interest group' case, the recipient agent acts on behalf of some narrow interest group, rather than in the interests of a broader political spectrum. In the ideal – though perhaps somewhat utopian – 'embedded' case, when the recipient principal and his agent(s) represent the same broader interests, the benefits derived from the reform depend on the fit between the proposed reform and the wider interest of the recipient country. If embeddedness is the case, then the donor has an interest in facilitating – rather than trying to prevent – post-contractual adjustment in the outputs of the project; that will only increase the benefits derived from the project by the beneficiary country. In the interest group case, the reverse is true and stricter monitoring will be required.

A peculiar situation arises in the case of EU aid for institutional reforms in its candidate member states in Central and Eastern Europe. There, the EU is not so much concerned with the welfare of the recipient country but rather the strict implementation of the *Acquis Communautaire*.[3] It may therefore seek an alliance with recipient country interest groups that share the EU's interest. Also, the contractor can be a non-profit organisation with a specific agenda, an interest group in its own right, that is willing to forgo some of the contractual rents in order to achieve its own agenda. This could

---

[3] The set of EU rules, regulations and directives to which all member states have to adhere.

be the case in so-called twinning projects under the EC-financed Phare technical assistance programme in candidate member states, where technical assistance is not normally provided by commercial companies but by government administrations from EU member states. The paper shows that the presence of interest groups and embeddedness multiplies the difficulties that donors have in ensuring that the independent contractors carry out their activities productively.

There is great paradox in the optimal configuration of the control of projects. If efficiency is the goal, contractors who are unfamiliar with a country should be given control of projects and contractors who are familiar with a country should be given less control. The paradox is resolved by noting that embeddedness implies that it is productive to stimulate bargaining between contractor and recipient.

From de jure *to* de facto *institutional reform in recipient countries*

Chapter 4, by Uwe Mummert, deals exclusively with institutional reform aid and the informational problems that it induces in principal–agent relationships in the recipient country. Whereas Murrell's paper examined how donor-financed contractors could achieve formal *de jure* reforms in recipient countries, Mummert examines what happens *de facto*, once the *de jure* reforms are approved.

'Normal' institutional reform processes are home-grown and the outcome of domestic economic, social and political forces. Donor-financed institutional reform projects transplant 'foreign' institutions into a domestic institutional setting. This includes cases such as International Monetary Fund (IMF)- and World-Bank-supported structural adjustment programmes, reforms related to membership of the World Trade Organisation (WTO), or transposition of the EU *Acquis* to candidate member states. For such reforms to be successful, the transferred institutions have to be not only *de jure* (formally) integrated into the formal institutions of the recipient country but also *de facto* embedded into the informal socio-economic institutions of the recipient society.

Effective institutional reform implies that *de jure* changes affect the *de facto* choices of the actors to whom the rules apply. Thus, it focuses on the 'embeddedness' of reforms in the wider socio-economic environment, the ties between society and government agents that are in charge of implementing reformed institutions, the power of informal institutions in social networks and how they might provide obstacles to effective institutional reforms.

The model developed in the paper distinguishes between two levels of principal–agent relationships in the recipient country. Political principals, who adopted the donor-induced institutional reform, delegate the task of implementation and verification to government agents, in return for a reward. As political principals are unable to observe all the actions of government agents, moral hazard may occur. These agents, in turn, give instructions to citizens to modify their behaviour in accordance with the new institutions. However, government agents do not operate in a social vacuum: they are embedded in social networks that include the citizens to whom they give instructions but who may also exercise various types of social and economic pressure on them. Citizens may informally influence the government enforcement agent through bribes or social sanctions. As a result, collusion of interests between enforcers and citizens and deviations from the intended outcome of the reform may occur. In order for legal *de jure* reform to be effective, legal sanctions must be strong enough to penetrate the inhibitive layer of informal non-legal sanctions. The model describes the mechanics of resistance to reforms and the cost–benefit calculations implied by these mechanics. Particular types and sources of resistance to reforms are explored: the tension between proscriptive and prescriptive content, co-operation–defection differentials and the extent of fragmentation in society.

Informal institutions are not inflexible and may also evolve as a result of reforms in formal institutions. As long as the net benefit from co-operation exceeds the benefit from defection, the new institution will be accepted. Assuming that co-operation–defection differentials are variable across a population, a sufficient condition for successful reform therefore would be to have a critical number of agents with positive co-operation–defection differentials. That lowers the cost of social sanctions for others so that their co-operation–defection differential becomes positive and compliance with the reform will gradually spread. The informal institutions that opposed it will disappear or be adapted. For example, as soon as the volume of private entrepreneurial activity reaches a critical mass, the rules and regulations that promote such enterprises will be gradually accepted in society.

The extent of segregation in society and entry barriers to segregated groups may also affect the effectiveness of reform. In highly fragmented societies, it is very difficult for economic actors to change groups in order to escape restraining informal institutions within their group. Fragmentation determines whether informal institutions that resist reform will be perceived as subordinate to the formal institutions, as well as the intensity of the impact of informal institutions on the dynamics of the market processes. Empirical research has shown that ethnic, linguistic and social fragmentation in society is indeed a significant determinant of economic development.

The role of evaluation in foreign aid performance

Finally, my own chapter – Chapter 5 – examines the informational problems in foreign aid programmes from a purely domestic angle. It focuses on the dichotomy between the objectives of two sources of domestic demand for foreign aid, taxpayers who have a genuine desire for wealth redistribution, and suppliers of aid services who are seeking business opportunities. While the first group attempts to maximise consumer surplus, the second are profit maximisers. The role of the domestic politician, as political head of the aid agency, is to try to marry both objectives in the implementation of the aid programme. Contrary to Murrell and Mummert (Chapters 3 and 4), I do not take into account the welfare objectives of the recipient country.

Because of the broken feedback loop between the beneficiaries and the donor country, the risk of moral hazard by aid services suppliers is very high. This can only be overcome by the introduction of an explicit information feedback mechanism: formal evaluation of aid programmes. For a given aid budget, there is an optimal share of that budget that should be spent on evaluation studies in order to maximise the impact of that budget. That optimal share strikes a balance between spending more money on aid projects to achieve objectives and spending more money on suppliers' supervision so as to ensure adequate performance for every unit of money spent on projects.

However, because evaluation is usually handled by the aid agency itself, it is subject to the politician's interest in keeping the middle ground between the opposing objectives of taxpayers and suppliers. Consequently, evaluation will be manipulated in function of these interests. Aid agencies and their political 'owners' have several instrumental variables at their disposal to do so. Firstly, they can reduce the share of the aid budget spent on evaluation. This eases performance pressure on suppliers and enhances their profit margins. On the other hand, it does of course reduce programme performance and thus consumer surplus for the taxpayers. Secondly, they can vary the quality of evaluations by manipulating the ratio of budget spent on evaluation data gathering to budget spent on projects. Lower-quality evaluation studies are defined as having larger standard deviations for the observations on project performance variables. With large standard deviations, confidence intervals become wider and it becomes more difficult to prove that a performance variable is off target. The final decision on budget share and quality of evaluations is determined by the composition of the political constituency that elected the politician. If taxpayers are predominant in that constituency, political principals will be inclined to increase spending on evaluation; if suppliers are predominant, the reverse will be true. Manipulation of the quality of evaluations allows politicians to drive a wedge between the interests of opposing constituencies, for instance in a coalition government. Less reliable reports satisfy suppliers because they make it more difficult to credibly criticise their performance; at the same time, it satisfies taxpayers' wishes to have performance feedback. Coalitions are not only held together by the glue of transfers but also by information smokescreens that veil opposing views and contradictory information.

In short, because of the broken 'natural' feedback loop in foreign aid, inserting an explicit evaluation function in foreign aid programmes is necessary to overcome moral hazard on behalf of aid services suppliers. But it is not a miracle solution to eliminate performance problems. Evaluation itself is subject to moral hazard, induced by the same institutional and political incentives that affect aid projects performance.

5. CONCLUSIONS

What lessons can we learn from these four studies? They show that the nature of foreign aid – with a broken information feedback loop – combined with the nature of public administrations (including aid agencies) in general – with multiple hard-to-measure objectives and often multiple principals too – put a number of inherent constraints on the performance of foreign aid programmes. All these constraints are due to imperfect information flows in the aid delivery process. Switching from investment-oriented towards institutional-reform-oriented aid programmes can make matters worse because the outputs of the latter are less tangible and therefore even more subject to information problems. Informed institutional design (of contracts, aid agreements, budget allocation mechanisms) can mitigate the impact of some of these informational constraints. However, most aid agencies and programmes work with fairly standardised institutional set-ups that leave little room for variation. Any deviations from the standard set-up are time-consuming, complex and costly to implement, unless there is a strong political will to go ahead. The range of foreign aid performance objectives that each type of aid agency can address with reasonable chances of success is limited. As most aid agencies intend to pursue a wide range of objectives and address an ever larger set of problems in strongly variable environments, they could usefully apply the findings of modern institutional economics and organisation theory so as to improve their performance and chances of success in meeting their objectives. Similarly, they would also benefit from accepting the – often political – limits to their range of effective actions. Making these limits more explicit would be an important step in that direction.

The models, techniques and interpretations developed here have wide application potential to all types of foreign aid institutions and organisations. Chapter 6 draws a number of policy conclusions, in terms of their applicability to different types of aid agencies. It uses the conclusions from the studies to demonstrate that careful canalisation of aid flows through different types of aid organisations – NGOs, bilateral and multilateral agencies – in relation to the objectives that donors and beneficiaries try to achieve, may improve aid performance by exploiting the inherent strengths and weaknesses of each type of aid organisation. Official bilateral aid may have advantages in fostering political and economic ties between donor and recipient countries. However, its internal incentive structure does not enable strong leverage on recipient country policies, especially not when collective action among donors is required: multilateral agencies may be in a better position there.

MDBs, although they are confronted with multiple principals too, tend to suffer less than multilateral grant donors from biased performance incentives. They operate mostly with money borrowed from capital markets, not fiscal revenue paid by taxpayers in member states. This may keep donors' commercial interests more at bay in decision-making. Also, since decision-making usually follows the majority principle, MDBs can forge coalitions among their multiple principals, both donors and beneficiaries, to implement policies that suffer less from the vagaries that are often associated with multiple principals. On the other hand, MDBs are banks and should ensure that their loan portfolio is serviced. This may force them to compromise on their conditionality stance.

NGOs are mostly focused on a narrow range of issues or even a single issue. NGO members usually hold a fairly coherent set of preferences that facilitates policy-making and implementation and makes them less subject to the problems of multiple objectives. Official bilateral aid agencies can delegate project implementation to NGOs to un-bundle their own multiple objectives into discrete projects with a narrower range of objectives. This relieves the official aid agency of some of the pressures and trade-offs induced by the pursuit of multiple objectives. It also facilitates a political consensus on the allocation of aid in the donor country. At the same time, the dependence of NGOs on official aid budgets gives official agencies control over the behaviour of NGOs and may temper their often strongly normative stance. NGOs trade organisational efficiency against the pursuit of normative objectives.

This research project has been successful in terms of its own objective to help explain the causes of persistent problems and behavioural patterns in EC foreign aid. It shows that the EC's predicament as a multilateral aid organisation is by no means exceptional in the world of foreign aid, that it is due to the incentives embedded in multilateral delegation of aid tasks, especially when that aid comes in the form of grants financed from tax revenue – as opposed to multilateral banks' loan-based aid – and decision-making is often subject to unanimity rules – as is the case in EU foreign policy and foreign aid. There are however, ways to improve this performance, mostly through granting more political autonomy to an independent EC aid agency and allowing majority voting in decision-making. It remains to be seen, of course, to what extent the findings of this research will be taken seriously and contribute to policy decisions.

This book is meant to be an original and innovative contribution to the debate on the performance of foreign aid programmes in general, and in particular on the role of the institutional set-up and incentives provided by the organisations that manage these programmes. It is certainly not the definitive view on that subject but may provide an encouragement for decision-makers in foreign aid to become more creative in the design of the institutional aspect of programmes and take into account the contributions that institutional economics can make to facilitate their mission.

This book has many shortcomings, the principal one being that it proves nothing. It puts forward possible interpretations of observed behaviour of foreign aid organisations, based on models derived from modern organisation theory. Examples are implanted in the text for illustrative purposes only and there is no attempt to empirically validate the models in a rigorous way. Doing so would require a substantial amount of data collection on the behaviour of aid organisations and agents within those organisations. Such an empirical exercise would go far beyond the presently available economic aggregates on foreign aid. It is hoped that this book provides some of the theoretical foundations that will stimulate empirical research and applications.

REFERENCES

Aghion, Ph. and Tirole, J. (1997) Formal and real authority in organisations. *Journal of Political Economy*, 105(1), 1–27.
Becker, G. (1983) A theory of competition among pressure groups for political influence. *Quarterly Journal of Economics*, 98(3), 371–400.

Boone, P. (1994) *The Impact of Foreign Aid on Savings and Growth*. Mimeo. London: London School of Economics.

Burnside, C. and Dollar, D. (1996) *Aid, Policies and Growth*. Policy Research Working Paper 1777. Washington DC: World Bank.

(2000) Aid, policies and growth. *American Economic Review*, 90(4), 847–68.

Carr, S. M., Eilish, 000, and MacLachlan, Malcolm (1998) *Psychology of Aid*. London: Routledge.

Clague, Ch. (ed.) (1998) *Institutions and Economic Development*. Baltimore: Johns Hopkins University Press.

Coase, R. (1937) The nature of the firm. *Economica*, 4, 386–405.

(1960) The problem of social cost. *Journal of Law and Economics*, 3, 1–44.

Collier, P., Guillaumont, P. and S., and Gunning, J.W. (1997) Redesigning conditionality. *World Development*, 25(9), 1399–1407.

Devarajan, S., Dollar D., and Holmgren, T. (1999) *Aid and Reform in Africa*. Draft summary report, World Bank Development Research Group working paper. Washington DC: World Bank.

Dixit, A. (1997) Power of incentives in private versus public organisations. *American Economic Review*, 87(2), 378–382.

Dollar, D. and Svensson, J. (1998) *What explains the success or failure of structural adjustment programs?* Mimeo. Washington DC: World Bank.

Downs, A. (1967) *Inside bureaucracy*. Rand Corporation research study. Boston, MA: Little & Brown.

European Commission (1997) *Phare Interim Evaluation Report*. EC Evaluation Unit. Brussels: European Commission. Available at http://www.europa.eu.int/comm/europeaid/evaluation

(1998) *Evaluation of aspects of EU Development Aid to the Mediterranean Region*. By Cowi, NEI and Andante. Brussels: European Commission. Available at http://www.europa.eu.int/comm/europeaid/evaluation

(2000) *The European Community External Co-operation Programmes: Policies, Management and Distribution*. Brussels: European Commission. Available at: http://www.europa.eu.int/comm/europeaid/evaluation

Frey, B., Horn, H., Persson, T., and Schneider, F. (1985) A formulation and test of a simple model of World Bank behaviour. *Weltwirtschaftliches Archiv*, 121(3), 438–447.

Furubotn, E. and Richter, R. (1998) *Institutions and Economic Theory: the contribution of the new institutional economics*. Ann Arbor, Michigan: University of Michigan Press.

Grossman, S. and Hart, O. (1986) The costs and benefits of ownership: a theory of lateral and vertical integration. *Journal of Political Economy*, 94, 691–719.

Haggard, S. and Webb, S. (eds.) (1994) *Voting for Reform: democracy, political liberalisation and economic adjustment*. New York: Oxford University Press.

Holmstrom, B. and Milgrom, P. (1991) Multitask principal–agent analyses: incentive contracts, asset ownership and job design. *Journal of Law, Economics and Organisation*, 7, 24–52.

Killick, T. (1995) A principal–agent analysis of conditionality – a reader's digest. London: Overseas Development Institute.

Laffont, J.J. and Tirole, J. (1993) *A Theory of Incentives in Regulation and Procurement*. Cambridge, MA: MIT press.

Martimort, D. (1991) *Multiple Principals as a Commitment Mechanism*. Mimeo. Toulouse: University of Toulouse.

Masten, S. and Williamson, O. (1999) *The Economics of Transaction Costs*. Cheltenham: Edward Elgar.

McCubbins, S. Noll, 000 and Weingast, 000 (1988) Administrative procedures as means of political control. *Journal of Law, Economics and Organisation*, 3(2), 243–278.

Mosley, P. (1997) Conditionality as a bargaining process: structural adjustment lending 1980–86. *Princeton Essays in International Finance*, 168.

Murshed, S. and Sen, S. (1995) Aid conditionality and military expenditure reduction in developing countries: models of asymmetric information. *Economic Journal*, 105, 498–509.

North, D. (1990) *Institutions, Institutional Change and Economic Performance*. Cambridge: Cambridge University Press.

Ostrom, E., Gibson, C., Shivakumar, S., and Andersson, K. (2001) *Aid, incentives and Sustainability: an institutional analysis of development co-operation*. Mimeo, produced for the Swedish International Development Agency, Workshop in Political Theory and Policy Analysis. Bloomington, IN: Indiana University.

Pietrobelli, C. and Scarpa, C. (1992) Inducing efficiency in the use of foreign aid, *Journal of Development Studies*, 29(1), 72–92.

Quarles van Ufford, P., Kruyt, D., and Downing, Th. (1988) *The Hidden Crisis in Development: Development Bureaucracies*. Amsterdam: Free University Press and United Nations University.

Ranis, G. and Mahmood, S. (1992) *The Political Economy of Development Policy Change*. Cambridge, MA: Blackwell.

Rodrik, D. (1997) *Why is There Multilateral Lending*. In the proceedings of the 1995 Annual Conference on Development Economics. Washington DC: World Bank.

Simon, H. and Barnard, Ch. (1958) *Administrative Behavior: a Study of Decision-Making Processes in Administrative Organization*. New York: Macmillan.

Streeten, P. (1988) Conditionality: a double paradox. In: *North-South Co-operation in Retrospect and Prospect*. London: Routledge.

Svensson, J. (1997) *When is Foreign aid Policy Credible*. Policy research working paper 1740. Washington DC: World Bank.

Tirole, J. (1994) The internal organisation of government. *Oxford Economic Papers*, 46, 1–29.

Tirole, J. (1999) Incomplete contracts: where do we stand? *Econometrica*, 67(4), 741–781.

Trombetta, M. (1992) Does conditionality help? An agency approach to conditional development aid. *Giornali Degli Economisti e Annali di Economia*, 51, 77–96.

Tsikata, T. (1998) *Aid Effectiveness: a Survey of Recent Empirical Literature.* Washington DC: IMF Paper on Policy Analysis, PPAA/98/1.

White, H. (1992) The macro-economic impact of development aid: a critical survey. *Journal of Development Studies*, 21(2), 163–240.

Williamson, O. (1985) *The Economic Institutions of Capitalism.* New York: Free press.

Whitman, D. (1995) *The Myth of Democratic Failure: Why Political Institutions are Efficient.* Chicago: University of Chicago Press.

World Bank (1997) *World Development Report* 1997. Washington DC: World Bank.

Conflicts of objectives and task allocation in aid agencies

Paul Seabright

1. INTRODUCTION: THE PROBLEM

Aid agencies differ from other organisations in the public and private sectors of society in a number of important ways, but most strikingly in that the people for whose benefit they are supposed to work are not the same as those from whom their revenues are obtained. Some people (taxpayers or private donors as the case may be) pay money directly or indirectly to the agency so that other people may benefit. This simple fact may seem unremarkable, but in reality it creates a strikingly difficult set of problems in institutional design.

Why should this be so? Other types of organisation, both public and private, carry out activities for the supposed benefit of those who pay them to do so. If the supposed beneficiaries are not happy with the benefits they receive they can protest – either by withdrawing their custom (if the organisation operates in a market), or by voting against the political authorities (if the organisation is controlled by a political process). In order to find out whether the benefits received are adequate given the costs, the beneficiaries need only consult themselves and their own preferences. Does this product yield good value for money? Are these public services worth the taxes we pay? Such interrogations of oneself are the stuff of daily life in all free societies.

Aid agencies are quite different. It sometimes happens that the sponsors – taxpayers or donors or both – judge an aid agency purely by its public pronouncements (as though the principal task of the agency were to deliver public pronouncements rather than to

The author greatfully acknowledges support for this study from the European Commission's Tacis programme.

deliver aid). But more often they are concerned to know to what extent the agency is doing the things that the supposed beneficiaries need. However, this is extremely difficult to evaluate, since there is frequently no obvious mechanism for transmitting the beneficiaries' view of the process to the sponsors. Instead the sponsors must rely on various indicators of performance. Some of these are easier to measure than others, and the relative weighting of each is extremely hard to assess and will typically differ from one sponsor to another. In other words, it is an intrinsic part of the predicament of aid agencies that they are subject to multiple conflicting criteria of evaluation. They perform multiple tasks, and they are answerable to multiple sponsors with differing evaluations of those tasks.

Note that the argument here is quite subtle. There is nothing unusual about the multiplicity of tasks: except in a trivial sense of the word 'task' any person in any organisation performs multiple tasks. But in many organisations these tasks result in an outcome which is evaluated by the person directly affected, who is therefore in the best position to judge the contribution of the different tasks to the overall result. In an aid agency, by contrast, the overall evaluation must be performed by someone who has only the outcomes of the different tasks to go on and who has only limited capacities to observe them. There is no clearly defined trade-off between various tasks and the goals to be accomplished – in contrast to private companies where profit is the single goal and the trade-off with various tasks is more easily measurable.

Is it surprising, then, that aid agencies frequently behave in ways that display an over-reliance on formal rules as against the exercise of sound judgement, a tendency to worry too much about meeting quantitative targets and not enough about the quality of the grants or loans they make? Is it any wonder that they pay too much attention to the performance of tasks that are easy to monitor, like the drunkard looking for his lost keys under a lamp-post because 'that's where the light is'? Is it remarkable that they pay more attention to the inputs to the aid process than to the outputs? And if the answer to some of these questions is 'no', is that inevitable given the intrinsic nature of aid agencies themselves, or is it something that intelligent organisational design could reasonably hope to avoid? This chapter seeks to shed light on some of these important questions.

The argument of the chapter proceeds through a number of steps. First, many aid agencies (although not all) are themselves public administrations, and suffer in consequence from problems characteristic of public administrations everywhere.[1] These include multiple objectives, the difficulty of measuring results, and consequently weak incentives for staff – including relatively fixed salaries and a dependence on internal promotion procedures that invite information manipulation to advance careers. Some valuable insights into these phenomena have been yielded by recent developments in principal–agent theory, which deals with the incentive issues that arise when there is a serious divergence of interest between those who perform tasks (agents) and those on whose behalf the tasks are performed (principals). The first task of the chapter is therefore to review some of the general insights of these theories.

Next, we consider the more particular problems of the European Union (EU) as an aid donor. These arise for three main reasons. Firstly, the European Commission (EC 'the EU's administrative body') is not exactly like any other public administration. It is answerable not to a single principal but to fifteen different national governments, with theoretical if not *de facto* parity of status. This leads to potential conflicts of priorities that exceed in degree those of other public administrations. Even the well-known conflicts between executive and legislature in countries such as the United States and (to a lesser extent) France do not involve the administration in the need to respond to pressures from quite so many different directions. Furthermore, none of the pressures come directly from the aid beneficiaries themselves, who have no feedback mechanism for influencing the behaviour of the donor except through the circuitous route of influencing the donor's own principals. Since the donor's principals care directly about the inputs into the aid process (contracts for consultants and for the supply of materials), but only indirectly about outputs (effects in the beneficiary countries), the various biases characteristic of public administrations will almost inevitably be more striking in the case of the EC than in public administrations of the more familiar kind.

---

[1] The rider is important. Aid agencies suffer from the problems identified here even when they are not public administrations, although the problems of public administrations in many circumstances aggravate those that are particular to aid agencies.

Secondly, although multilateral aid agencies share this predicament of answerability to multiple principals, the EC is not quite like other aid agencies either. Political oversight in multilateral agencies, such as the World Bank or the International Monetary Fund (IMF) is typically exercised through executive boards, which are intermediary fora where there is at least some attempt to form coherent objectives through repeated interaction, and which are composed of full-time representatives of the member governments. The governments' often expressed anxiety that their representatives 'go native' is precisely testimony to the fact that they seek compromises in the interest of a more coherent overall policy. But the main pressure on EC accountability comes through the Council, which is composed of serving politicians whose main focus is on their domestic interests. They spend too little time on EC affairs to come under any significant pressure to 'go native' (a criticism that tends to be confined to full-time Commissioners rather than part-time Council Members).

Thirdly, a combination of budgetary pressures and the intrinsic character of the challenges involved mean that a large part of the EC's external aid programme has taken the form of technical assistance for the purpose of fostering institutional reform. Success and failure in this area are notoriously hard to measure even by the standards of aid programmes elsewhere, a fact that has profound consequences (as we shall see) for the nature of the work the EC can reasonably be expected to carry out.

The difficulties faced by the EC in the management of its aid programmes have been well documented, and have indeed acquired considerable notoriety recently. To some extent, a focus on questions of fraud and illegality can divert attention from other difficulties, such as the extent to which EC aid is achieving its objectives (a characteristic of the output of the process rather than its inputs). Indeed, to the extent that a focus on inputs may worsen the quality of scrutiny of outputs, procedures designed to tackle fraud or illegality might make some of the difficulties described above more severe. The recent Report of the Committee of Independent Experts (1999) says, for instance, of the appointment of M. Berthelot by Commissioner Cresson that 'the work performed was manifestly deficient in terms of quantity, quality and relevance. The Community did not get value for money', but recommends that 'the human resources allocated to internal auditing be greatly increased', a measure that increases attention to financial accuracy without doing anything to augment quality, relevance or value for money. The overall impact of such measures will depend to a considerable extent on whether scrutiny of inputs and scrutiny of outputs complement or substitute for one another in the day-to-day work of aid officials.

Are such problems avoidable? It is striking that the more general complaints made about EC aid echo across studies of aid agencies everywhere, in kind if not always in degree (see Cassen *et al.*, 1994).[2] This suggests that comparative evaluations of different agencies may help to illuminate the extent to which such problems are inevitable, and the extent to which they may be capable of being resolved by intelligent organisational design. A particularly interesting and thorough documentation occurs in a number of studies of the World Bank, as well as in the Bank's own Oral History Program.[3] The case of the World Bank is all the more telling since it has enjoyed more than most agencies an access to high-quality technical expertise and has been subject to a need to justify its performance before sceptical national shareholders. The Bank's case is particularly interesting for the EC because of the nature of its answerability to multiple member governments; it should not surprise us if the phenomena uncovered in the Bank studies appear in the EC to an even greater degree.

The extent to which the measurability of success and failure determined priorities is a recurring theme of the Bank studies. Mason and Asher (1973), for example, note that:

the Bank recognized [during its first twenty-five years] that investments of many kinds were needed for development but frequently implied that one kind was more essential than any other . . . projects to develop electric power and transport facilities were accordingly considered especially appropriate for Bank financing. At the same time the Bank was led to eschew certain fields traditionally open to public investment, even in the highly-developed free-enterprise economies: namely, sanitation, education, and

---

[2] The question whether aid works has of course spawned a vast literature, much of which qualitatively supports the kinds of observation made here, but which differs according to whether the authors regard this state of affairs as inevitable or deplorable. See, for example, Chambers (1983), Lal (1983), Browne (1990), Lele (1990); Lipton and Toye (1990); Mosley, *et al.* (1991).

[3] Mason and Asher (1973), Kapur *et al.* (1997).

health facilities. Investments in these so-called 'social overhead' fields were widely considered to be as fundamental to development as are investments in hydroelectric sites, railroads, highways and 'economic overhead' programs. The contribution of social overhead projects to increased production, however, is less measurable and direct than that of power plants (Mason and Asher, 1973, pp.189, 150).

When one senior bank official was asked in 1961: 'Doesn't it really in fact turn out that the Bank . . . puts a great emphasis on specific projects partly for public relations reasons and partly . . . to satisfy the market . . . [that] the Bank's bonds are tied to something physical which can be seen and pointed to thereafter[?]', he replied 'Yes, I would agree?'.[4]

This is not to say that the Bank has only recently paid attention to the less tangible sides of development. For example, although 'institution-building' is often thought of as a recent fashion, it has been a central component of many World Bank loan agreements since the early 1950s (Kapur *et al.*, 1997 vol. 1, p.103). Nevertheless, it was typically a component of a project that had been selected for its overall ease of monitoring – and in the implementation it was easy for that component to be overlooked except insofar as it contributed to the aggregate measurable outcome.

What has changed substantially over time is that the targets and aims of Bank lending have multiplied. Writing of the 1980s and early 1990s, Kapur *et al.* say:

Meanwhile, trying to enforce multiple preconditioned policy targets was sapping the seriousness of the Bank's adjustment lending. It was a kind of Catch-22. Targets had been added to adjustment exercises because they were good causes and it was administratively easy to do. But procedurally the choice had been for pre-conditioning: borrowers entered into fairly precise contracts to do or not to do things that were sufficiently measurable for nonperformance to be conspicuous. Review after review of adjustment lending wrung its hands over the proliferation of borrowers' agreed undertakings. In the Second (1990) Review of Adjustment Lending (RAL) . . . the number of undertakings per adjustment loan was up to fifty-six, and it continued to rise. There was no way so many simultaneous agreements could be monitored, let alone enforced (Kapur *et al.*, 1997, vol. 1, p.30).

---

[4] Cope, Oral History, 1961, cited in Kapur *et al.* (1997, vol. 1, p.124).

At the same time as having to undertake multiple tasks evaluated according to multiple criteria, the Bank has been answerable to multiple constituencies. Many particular loans have been made – or blocked – because of pressure from shareholder governments. To take some early examples, Kapur *et al.* (1997) note nine World Bank loans to Nicaragua between 1951 and 1956 due to the 'highly convenient' relationship between Washington and the Somoza family[5]; the fact that 'a loan to Iraq was rushed through the Board in 1950 [because] British relations with Iraq, and access to its oil, were at stake'; the reversal in 1956 under US pressure of an earlier decision not to open a line of export credit to Iran; and continued obstacles to lending to Indonesia because of Dutch objections to its expropriations of foreign assets (Kapur *et al.*, 1997, pp. 104–106).

These examples suggest that even multilateral aid agencies can reproduce within themselves some of the problems of co-ordination that have been noted by Cassen *et al.* (1994, p. 184) for the separate activities of bilateral donors. They argue that the obstacles to co-ordination between donors are that:

- 'co-ordination is likely to impair the freedom with which donors can pursue their commercial and political interests through their aid programmes'
- 'donors know there are subjects on which they are likely to disagree, particularly in the matter of development policies'
- 'co-ordination can be costly in administrative time and expense'.

The consequence is a 'proliferation of aid projects and of equipment types . . . The results of this are very commonly a large number of projects which the recipient is ill-equipped to manage'. If this is true of the actions of bilateral donors it is also true of the outcome of the pressures exerted on multilateral agencies by their multiple constituencies. Nevertheless, such agencies can often do better than bilateral ones in precisely the areas where procedures are open to easy monitoring – for example, in the implementation of 'relatively transparent and internationally competitive bidding procedures for procurement'.[6]

---

[5] See Lake (1989), p. 103.   [6] Cassen *et al.* (1994), p. 205.

None of these observations necessarily imply (and none are intended by their authors to imply) that aid agencies are necessarily falling below some reasonable standard of behaviour. These features of their procedures may be the inevitable predicament of a large bureaucracy whose sponsors are not its beneficiaries (a description would encompass large non-governmental organisations as well as public aid administrations). But how can we assess such a claim, and what scope for organisational improvement might such a claim concede? To answer this question it is necessary to look more closely at recent developments in the economic theory of organisational design.

Although it is nearly a century since Max Weber first introduced bureaucracy as a serious subject of study, the formal analysis of bureaucratic organisations (including both large firms and non-market organisations) is still in a very underdeveloped state.[7] It forms part of the more general theory of incentives under asymmetric information, that is of circumstances where individuals need to be motivated to act in certain ways even though their actions cannot be perfectly monitored and enforced. The reason why the formal theory is still underdeveloped is that is still young. It dates from the 1970s, and has come to be known as principal-agent theory. It considers the relation between one party (a principal) who has an interest in the performance of a certain task (such as the management of a firm, the farming of a piece of land, the undertaking of a bureaucratic task) – and a second party (an agent), who has to undertake the task directly and must be motivated to do so in the principal's interest. In the case of aid agencies we can think of two types of principal–agent problem: one is that the administrators have to be motivated to work in the interests of the funders. The other is that both funders and administrators claim to be working in the interests of the ultimate beneficiaries, but need to be given credible incentives to do so. Finding the right incentives is at the heart of the principal–agent problem.

Principal–agent theory has yielded some powerful insights in many applications, but its usefulness for the study of bureaucracy has only just begun to be explored. Its early applications were to

---

[7] Though see Downs (1967) for a readable and interesting account of bureacracies.

circumstances where the principal had simple and clear goals (profit or output, say), and the other party (an agent) had to undertake a single task. The focus was therefore on the intrinsic effects of the divergence of interests between the parties, in the presence of asymmetric information. However, most large bureaucracies have to undertake a range of tasks, and many pursue what are in effect multiple goals, as the discussion above of the EC's predicament has illustrated. Yet as many of the most interesting incentive problems arise precisely in large organisations, it has been common to draw inferences from simpler models, without any rigorous basis for knowing when such conclusions are likely to be robust.

More recent work in the theory of incentives has been exploring the consequences of relaxing the various limiting assumptions of the simple principal–agent model. The next section of the paper will review the literature on multiple agents, and the literature on multiple principals, which is the formal way of representing the predicament of an agency subject to conflicting pressures from many constituencies. These multiple principals could be thought of as the different shareholders of the World Bank, or the fifteen member states of the EU who impose multiple pressures on their common agent the EC. Then I shall consider an issue closer to the problem under investigation, namely the question what happens when a principal requires the performance of multiple tasks. A recent important paper by Dewatripont *et al.* (2000) will be described in some detail, and then I shall develop a model designed to capture some phenomena that Dewatripont *et al.* do not consider. These will turn out to be of particular importance for organisations that have to decide the emphasis to be given to several tasks in the context of developing a career structure for the agents concerned.

Two particular features characterise the problem of how to perform multiple interdependent tasks – that is, tasks in which the performance of one is affected by how well the other is performed, either because the two tasks compete for the time or other inputs supplied by the agent or because one of them is in some sense an input into the other (that is, they may be substitutes or complements).

Firstly, the tasks may differ in the ease with which their performance can be monitored – one might require simply financial indicators while the other might require overall impact assessments.

We have already noted how pervasive has been this problem in the activities of the EC and the World Bank, and other agencies are little different even if the phenomenon has yet to be so minutely documented.

Secondly, the interdependence of these tasks means that incentives for the performance of one will affect the performance of the other. Under some circumstances, the more thoroughly the second task is performed the harder it will be to perform the first. For example, one task may be the preparation of grant or loan proposals, while the second may be the screening of the same proposals. The more rigorous the screening the fewer proposals may be left to go through. Under other circumstances, though, the performance of one task may enter positively into the production function of the other. For example, the first task may be institution-building while the second is the operation of some physical infrastructure: the better the first task is performed the easier it may be to perform the second. In this example, the first task is the harder to monitor but the converse is also often observed. The first task might consist of supply of some physical inputs while the second consists of operating those inputs in a way consistent with the needs of beneficiaries: the first can be observed quite precisely while the satisfactory performance of the second is much harder to establish. Indeed, one possible explanation for the so-called 'inputs bias' in the implementation of aid programmes may be that this latter structure of aid tasks is more common than the former.

While as a general rule these features are simply given by the intrinsic nature of the task concerned, there may be circumstances where a given ultimate objective (poverty alleviation, say) can be accomplished with more than one structure of tasks, in which case the particular character of the complementarity or substitutability of tasks becomes a matter of choice for the organisation concerned. For example, one consequence of the use of compensation in kind rather than in cash for tribal groups resettled as a consequence of the Narmada dam project in North-Western India has been a typically low quality of land available for resettlement. As Satyanarayana (2000) reports, this has been because requiring government agencies to be responsible for disbursement of (easily monitored) budgetary outlays as well as for the quality of land purchase (which is hard to monitor) has led them to devote disproportionate attention to the former task at the expense of the latter. In these circumstances cash compensation (which allows the individuals to be responsible for their own land purchase and enables government officials to concentrate on a simpler task structure) would have been preferable.

To summarise, this paper is structured as follows. Section 2 reviews the literature on multiple agents, and the literature on multiple principals. Section 3 discusses the nature of multiple tasks and describes a model due to Dewatripont *et al.* (2000). Section 4 outlines the main model of this paper. Section 5 concludes.

2. MULTIPLE AGENTS AND MULTIPLE PRINCIPALS

The costs of delegation

One of the main findings of the principal–agent literature is that in the presence of asymmetric information between the principal and the agent there will be unavoidable costs of delegation of a task – costs over and above the minimum necessary to compensate the agent for the effort of undertaking the task in the first place. These costs fall into two broad categories.

Firstly, when there is moral hazard (the agent cannot commit to an efficient action), the agent will have to be exposed to more risk than would otherwise be desirable, in order to give enough incentive to work in the principal's interests. The agent will therefore need to be compensated by a higher average payment than would be necessary under complete information, as compensation for the additional risk. Thus the director of an agency may have to resign if the agency fails to meet its targets, even if it cannot be demonstrated that this was the fault of the director; the director needs to be given an incentive to lower the risk of such an eventuality even if it cannot be altogether eliminated.

Secondly, when there is adverse selection (the agent has private information prior to signing the contract) the principal must give the agent an incentive to reveal this information correctly. This constitutes an informational rent, which lowers the return to the principal compared with what would be received under complete information. Thus, for example, expatriate employees of an international agency may need to be given standard 'hardship allowances' for foreign postings even if in some postings they may be substantially better off as a result – otherwise they will have an incentive to exaggerate the hardship of the particular circumstances they face.

It is by now well known (Mookherjee, 1984) that when several agents work on behalf of one principal, these delegation costs can be reduced if the principal takes account of any correlation in the uncertainty faced by different agents. The way this can be achieved is by using 'yardstick' performance comparisons. For example, 'yardstick regulation' uses the correlation between the shocks affecting the production costs of several regulated firms to devise rules for determining the movement of a price cap. A firm is rewarded not for its absolute success in reducing costs but for its success relative to the costs of other firms.[8] Similarly, comparison between the performance of different project directors in somewhat similar circumstances may make it easier to tell to what extent adverse performance on any one project was due to bad luck as opposed to bad management. If one project did badly while others facing similar shocks did well it is more likely to be a failure of management. Another example is the presence of a number of different agencies answerable to a major general organisation such as the United Nations (UN): recent management failures in the United Nations Educational, Scientific and Cultural Organisation (UNESCO) were able to be addressed by pointing to the fact that these were not the inevitable consequence of being a UN agency, as the superior performance of other UN agencies demonstrated.

Whereas the presence of multiple agents has a fairly unambiguous effect on improving information flows (subject to the costs of administration and information processing), the presence of multiple principals has a more complex effect. Many interesting issues arise when an agent works on behalf of more than one principal. This may happen in one of two main ways:

(a) **Hierarchy**. A principal delegates a task to an agent who further delegates the task or some part of it to a subordinate. In this

---

[8] See Armstrong *et al.* (1994).

case the agent can be thought of as acting also as a principal with respect to the subordinate. This is a very common predicament for all large organisations, most of whose members are simultaneously seeking to provide incentives for their subordinates while themselves responding to the incentives of their superiors.

(b) **Joint delegation**. An agent works directly on behalf of two or more principals, each of whom has an interest in some dimension of the work performed by the agent, and the agent's performance in one dimension influences his incentives for performance in another. The situation of the EC's new Common Service is a case in point, but all the EU institutions are in some sense the result of joint delegation by the member states.

Most organisations of any degree of complexity contain elements of both hierarchy and joint delegation. We consider these in turn.

Hierarchy

There are three main ways in which the incentives in a hierarchy differ from those in a simple bilateral principal–agent relationship.

The chain of delegation
Firstly, there is a longer 'chain of delegation', which means there is – potentially – an efficiency loss at each stage in the chain, and the incentives of those further down the chain are further and further removed from those of the principal. Consider the following examples. The sponsors of an aid agency delegate its management to directors. But the directors cannot carry out all the tasks themselves so delegate them to subordinate staff. The directors seek to ensure staff act in the directors' rather than the sponsors' interests. Alternatively, citizens delegate political action to elected representatives. The latter delegate it to a government. Scrutiny of the governments' actions is carried out by MPs rather than the citizens directly.

Here it is worth noting that the feature of aid agencies described at the start of this paper has a radical implication. Aid beneficiaries are not part of the constituency of the political owners of the aid agency: the chain of delegation is broken. Only the firms and consultants who provide inputs into aid programmes are part of that constituency, and this fact will strengthen any pre-existing inputs bias in aid.

Intermediaries to enhance strategic credibility
Secondly, the principal can use an intermediary (a 'manager') to enforce a more credible set of incentives for the agent than the agent would be able to implement alone. This is potentially beneficial to the principal. Note that sometimes the way in which this mechanism is made credible is through joint delegation with another principal, so hierarchy and joint delegation may reinforce each other in this respect.

For example, a multilateral agency may be able to resist pressure to make loans for purely political purposes than would the aid arm of a single country. The World Bank examples given above suggest that this will not always be successful (though they may also illustrate the dangers of having one or two dominant shareholders as opposed to a more balanced allocation of power). Nevertheless, Cassen *et al.* (1994, p.215) conclude that on balance multilateral agencies 'are largely apolitical' compared to bilateral donors. However, this conclusion appears more reasonable for those multilateral agencies that have genuinely delegated their management to an executive board than for those (like the EC) where responsibility rests in the hands of serving politicians from member states. One lesson may be that more genuinely devolved control may be necessary to diminish the extent of politicisation of EC aid (or, more accurately, of influence by the commercial interests of member states). Alternatively, multilateral agencies may be able credibly to implement reasonably competitive and non-discriminatory procedures for tendering and procurement. EC experience suggests this may be easier (because it can be enforced by easily monitored auditing procedures) than diminishing politicisation in the choice of projects and beneficiaries[9] – another revealing instance of inputs bias at work.

---

[9] Indeed, the Committee of Independent Experts (1999) has noted that 'internal auditing . . . is generally satisfactory', while 'a priori control [which] is embodied in the approval procedure . . . is very ineffective'.

Manipulation by intermediaries

Thirdly, an intermediary can use the terms under which the agent is monitored in a strategic manner to improve their ability to extract concessions from the principal. This is potentially costly to the principal. It is likely to occur whenever the manager does not just play a role in a contract with the agent determined by the principal, but also has some influence over the terms of that contract.

For example, if the agent could be motivated by some combination of incentive payments and direct monitoring by the manager, the manager may choose more monitoring than is necessary, in order to increase his indispensability to the principal (Anderlini, 1990). This may explain a tendency for aid organisations to be unnecessarily large from the point of view of their sponsors' interests. It also accounts for some of the phenomena described in Murrell (Chapter 3), where contractors influence the terms of an aid contract to increase their own rent.

Again, if recruitment of the agent is the responsibility of a manager in an organisation, the latter may deliberately recruit low-quality people to prevent them from being promoted above him. Alternatively the manager may tend to avoid recruiting or rewarding those with scarce technical skills, whose promotion may be particularly difficult to prevent. One way of resolving this difficulty is through the use of seniority-based promotion systems: these can be seen as a form of commitment device designed to reassure managers that they will not be threatened by recruiting high quality workers. In bureaucracies where the performance of workers is hard for senior management to monitor, and where they must depend on intermediate management for this information, this means that relatively inflexible seniority-based promotion systems are likely to be particularly common. This will somewhat mitigate, but will not avoid altogether, the adverse recruitment incentives just described.

Joint delegation

This occurs when an agent works in common for more than one principal. In addition to the obvious examples cited above, such as the answerability of the EC to 15 member states, joint delegation also occurs within large organisations. For example, the Commission has created a Common Service to manage the implementation of aid projects originating in several different Directorates-General. Joint delegation differs rather obviously from simple delegation in that the actions taken by the various principals to motivate the agent may impose externalities on each other. This is likely to result in various inefficiencies, ranging from simple confusion over priorities to more systematic instances where the agent pursues a series of narrow goals instead of a coherent broad goal.[10] For instance, an aid agency might fund a large number of inefficiently small projects to satisfy its various donors in turn rather than a smaller number of large ones. So why should it ever be in the interest of the principals to undertake joint delegation? What could be the compensating advantages (Neven *et al.*, 1998)?

Co-ordination

The principals may be able to use the agent to co-ordinate their actions in a way that they are prevented from doing directly. One example from industrial economics is when the principals are two firms that are not allowed either to merge, to co-ordinate their pricing behaviour or directly to share markets (because of competition law). Nevertheless, by using a joint distributor (for example) they can effectively ensure that this distributor co-ordinates their pricing and shares the market on their behalf (see Bernheim and Whinston, 1986).

In the context of aid agencies, for example, bilateral agencies may come under strong political pressure to use aid as a means of furthering competition for recipient countries' markets. A joint agency may be able to commit more credibly not to seek to do so; though, as the discussion above emphasised, it may not be easy to make this commitment stick.

Another example is provided by instances where aid is tied to some general political goal that has multiple interpretations (such as the furtherance of democracy). A multilateral agency may be able

---

[10] More precisely, the agents' actions are not even constrained (second-best) efficient – they do not even maximise the joint surplus of the principals subject to the constraints of asymmetric information.

to commit to avoid using aid to further particular political interest groups within the donor countries and concentrate instead on supporting more open political processes. The charter of the European Bank for Reconstruction and Development, for instance, includes a commitment to the furtherance of democracy, whereas many individual countries' aid programmes have been strongly tied to the fortunes of particular political parties. However, the example of Russia makes clear that multilateralism did not shield the IMF and World Bank from considerable pressure to make loans to support President Yeltsin. Again the problem may lie with insufficient multilateralism rather than with multilateralism *per se*.

Commitment to the agent's incentives

The presence of one principal may be a means whereby the other principal can commit to an incentive structure for the agent that would otherwise not be credible. For example, a bilateral donor that tried to commit itself to using competitive and non-discriminatory procurement policies might come under heavy political pressure to favour its own suppliers, especially if domestic interest groups could claim that other countries were not doing the same. But the same commitment may be much easier to make for a multilateral agency, since each country can argue to its domestic interest groups that other countries insist upon non-discriminatory procedures. All countries may be collectively better off if such a commitment is reached (there is less waste in the overall aid budget), even if each country on its own has an interest in trying to favour its own suppliers.

Inefficiency as an ex post threat

The inefficiency of joint delegation can be used as a threat to give the agent a strategic advantage in negotiating with a third party (Martimort, 1993). When President Clinton obtained 'fast-track' authority to negotiate a General Agreement on Tariffs and Trade (GATT) deal, this was time-limited so that other countries had an incentive to reach an agreement quickly, for fear of authority reverting to Congress (a set of multiple principals).

In another example, aid initiatives may be dispersed between agencies rather than concentrated in the hands of a single super-agency, in order to make capture by special interest groups more difficult. So various UN agencies in charge of children, health and so on may face problems of co-ordination, but this may be thought preferable to undue concentration of power in the hands of a single agency.

Economies of scope

There may be important economies of scope between the activities performed for one principal and the tasks required by another. To get two agents to do the job would involve wasteful duplication of activity. However, the sharing of tasks creates some significant distortionary incentives. This is particularly true where the principals are not of the same kind (for instance, several member states), but rather involve quite different kinds of principal (for instance, a donor political authority and a set of beneficiaries, or a set of tax-payers and a set of consumers). One familiar day-to-day example of this kind of problem in joint delegation occurs in the medical profession, where doctors act simultaneously as agents for their patients and for whoever is paying for the treatment (typically an insurance company or the State). For the latter the doctor must certify the patient's state of health and therefore the level of resour-ces to which the patient's insurance contract entitles him. For the patient himself the doctor must give advice as to the best way of regaining health given the resources available. The former task creates incentives for under-diagnosis, the latter for over-diagnosis. This analogy is very apt to aid agencies, for like doctors agencies work for the benefit of those who are typically not their paymasters.

Specifically, agencies typically act to report on the objective need for funding of various beneficiary countries. This is true not just in the high-profile cases of famine and natural disaster, where the reports of agencies on the scene are often the only available infor-mation about the scale of the disaster. More mundanely, it is the reports of agencies from their projects 'on the ground' that provide the basis under which appeals for funds are made (to the public or to the political authorities).

Agencies also, and obviously, act to further the interests of the aid beneficiaries. This is entirely proper, though it also creates incentives to lobby on behalf of the beneficiaries in respect of appeals for funds. And to the extent that agencies' budgets are dependent on the outcome of such lobbying, it makes agencies into natural allies of those who would exaggerate the objective funding needs in particular cases.[11]

Insofar as they act as agents of their sponsors, agencies may have an incentive to downplay the scale of difficulties in the beneficiary countries. Insofar as they act as agents of the beneficiaries they may have an incentive to exaggerate them (this has been a persistent theme of critics of foreign aid on the political right). Even if it might be better for sponsors and beneficiaries to have separate agencies representing them, the duplication of effort this would require would be thoroughly wasteful.

As this example indicates, assessing the efficiency of joint delegation is no easy matter, since it typically involves a trade-off between benefits (such as economies of scope, or improved credibility of commitments) and costs in the form of imperfect internalisation of the externalities between the principals. If we consider either solely the costs or solely the benefits it is easy to gain a misleading impression of the overall character of the joint delegation relationship.

A contrasting problem: multiple tasks

In the next section we consider a much more recent development of the simple principal–agent model, namely the extension to the case where the agent can potentially perform a multiplicity of tasks, but where some of these tasks are much more straightforward to monitor than others. This predicament arises in all large bureaucracies, and in that sense is by no means peculiar to aid agencies. But it arises in aid agencies in a particularly strong form, as we shall see. This is because aid agencies face even greater problems with monitoring the quality of work, because of the lack of direct feedback from beneficiaries in their structure of command and responsibility. This lack of feedback enhances the input bias that has already been discussed.

[11] De Waal (1998) is a strong statement of this point.

The basic foundations of this model draw on two sets of ideas. Firstly, there is the 'career concerns' model of Holmstrom (1982), which shows what happens when agents are motivated not by direct monetary rewards but by the hope of demonstrating their abilities to some kind of professional labour market. This is particularly applicable to the case of aid agencies whose staff tend to be salaried rather than paid in a manner directly linked to ostensible performance. Secondly, there is the multi-task model of Holmstrom and Milgrom (1991), which demonstrates that when tasks compete for an agent's time and attention, incentives for the performance of one may affect the performance of the other. Specifically, incentives for easily-monitored tasks will need to be less high-powered than they would be in a single-task model, in order to avoid diverting the agent's effort away from other tasks. Indeed, this is the principal justification of paying agency staff fixed salaries: if not they would tend to focus on those aspects of the job that affected their salaries to the exclusion of other, perhaps more important tasks. As it is, the easily-monitored tasks tend to be those that involve the inputs into the aid process; the output-related tasks tend to be relatively hard to monitor. The presence of input bias in the aid process would almost certainly be exacerbated if agency staff were not paid fixed salaries. The model of the next section takes this idea a stage further by considering the determinants of a (constrained) optimal allocation of tasks.

3. A MODEL OF MULTIPLE TASKS

In this section we present the outline of a multi-task principal–agent model, due to Dewatripont *et al.* (2000). In this model the principal is taken to represent either an organisation or a market that is interested in the talent revealed by an agent's actions, and will reward the agent according to the value of that talent (insofar as it can be inferred from observed behaviour). It is assumed that the agent is assigned to work on some number n of tasks (one of the purposes of the model is to show how the incentives for effort vary with the number of tasks). The agent begins by choosing an unobservable vector of costly actions $a = (a_1, \ldots, a_n)$, incurring private cost $c(a)$, and yielding a vector of observable outcomes

$y = (y_1, \ldots, y_n)$. The result is a reward t to the agent, whose utility is this reward minus the cost of his actions $t - c(a)$.

This reward reflects the market's expectation of the agent's talent Θ. Dewatripont *et al.* show that in equilibrium, the marginal cost of the agent's actions will be set equal to the covariance of talent and the likelihood ratio. Put simply, this means that effort is higher when observed behaviour is more informative about the agent's talent.

Using this basic result, Dewatripont *et al.* go on to show (*inter alia*) the following three points:

(a) When only the aggregate performance on all n tasks together is observable, equilibrium total effort is decreasing in the number of tasks entrusted to the agent. They interpret this as implying a 'benefit from focus', in that the performance of a more limited number of tasks increases the ability of the market to infer talent from performance.

(b) In addition, under certain conditions governing the interaction of talent and effort, even when the agent focuses on a single task, effort is higher when the market knows exactly which task this is rather than having to infer it from observable outcomes. The authors interpret this as implying the superiority of giving clear rather than 'fuzzy' missions to bureaucratic organisations. In the context of aid agencies it can also be interpreted to mean that a degree of input bias is unavoidable, since clear missions are easier to define with respect to inputs (budgetary allocations, finance, contracts, experts) than with respect to outputs (project outcomes and impact).

(c) When tasks require different talents, it is better to group together tasks that require similar talents. This is interpreted as implying that it is better to employ specialists than generalists.

The results of Dewatripont *et al.* are important and original, but they have one particular limitation. They demonstrate the benefits of specialisation and of precision in bureaucratic organisation, but they ignore their costs. Taken literally, their paper would imply, for example, that if only aggregate performance measures were available, each agent should undertake only a single task. Given that tasks for this purpose can be defined as narrowly as we please, this would imply a degree of specialisation against which Fordist production techniques would seem like dilettantism. And it would certainly imply that all aid agencies ever seen have been utterly disastrously structured for the nature of the tasks in hand.

So it is important to develop the insights of these authors by considering the nature of the trade-offs that have to be made in bureaucratic task design: what are the costs of specialisation to be set against the benefits? Describing this trade-off is the main task of the model in the next section. There we shall take seriously the idea that different tasks require different talents. However, talents may be correlated, and the performance on different tasks may be complementary. So too much specialisation is costly for two reasons. Firstly, it does not exploit the fact that an agent who is good at one task may be good at another task that is complementary to the first. Secondly, it does not use the information revealed by performance on one task about the agent's talent for the other: in an organisation that seeks to use performance as a guide to promotion this information will be valuable. The model will therefore be one with two periods, rather artificially distinguished so that in the second, information is valuable purely for intrinsic task performance, while in the first it is also valuable for promotion.

4. A MODEL OF MULTIPLE TALENTS

In this section we present a simple model with multiple talents as well as multiple tasks. Unlike the model of the previous section it has two periods, thereby allowing us to examine not only the incentive problem in any given period but also the selection problem when a principal uses the agent's performance in the first period to determine whom to employ in the second. These two problems turn out to be interrelated, in that because promotion is desirable, the criteria of selection determine both the distribution of talent in the second period and the choice of effort in the first. In the context of aid agencies, the model therefore casts light both on the extent to which they concentrate effort on some tasks rather than others, but also on the kinds of skills and talents they seek to employ and the nature of the individuals they promote.

There is a single risk-neutral principal and a pool of risk-neutral agents. Adding risk aversion to the model would complicate the calculations without adding new insight. There are two tasks to be undertaken; each agent may undertake both tasks, or the agents may be allocated to them separately (not necessarily in equal proportions). We discuss below some interpretations of these tasks in the context of aid agencies; the model shows when it will be preferable to separate and when to bundle the tasks. Each task requires both talent and effort. In addition, output of the second task is potentially affected by the performance of the first. We can think of this as implying that the first good is an input into the production of the second, though it may not only be an input, in that it may also be valued in its own right. This is particularly significant in the context of aid agencies, because it is well known that donors care about the benefits to their own contractors (consultants or suppliers of procured goods).

The tasks may be performed separately (one agent assigned to each task), or both agents may be required to perform both tasks. Formally, we write the production function for the input task as:

$$y_1 = \alpha_1 \cdot a_1 \cdot c_1 \qquad (2.1)$$

while that for the output task is:

$$y_2 = \alpha_2 \cdot a_2 \left(b \cdot y_1 + c_2 \right) \qquad (2.2)$$

where α_i is the talent of the agent undertaking task i, a_i is the effort of the agent in the performance of task i, and b, c_1 and c_2 are constants.

When the tasks are performed together by both agents, the production function becomes (by substitution of (2.1) in (2.2)):

$$y_2 = \alpha_2 \cdot a_2 \left(b \cdot \alpha_1 \cdot a_1 \cdot c_1 + c_2 \right) \qquad (2.3)$$

Each agent is endowed with talents represented by an ordered pair (α_1, α_2). Both α_1 and α_2 are assumed to have a uniform (rectangular) probability density bounded below by α_L and bounded above by α_H. However, their distributions may be correlated, and indeed the extent of the correlation plays an important part in the conclusions of the model.

Neither the talent of the agents nor the output they produce is directly observable in the first period before the end of the game.

Instead the outputs y_1 and y_2 are observed with a random error, so we can write:

$$\tilde{y}_1 = y_1 + \varepsilon_1 = \alpha_1 \cdot a_1 \cdot c_1 + \varepsilon_1 \qquad (2.4)$$

and:

$$\tilde{y}_2 = y_2 + \varepsilon_2 = \alpha_2 \cdot a_2 \left(b \cdot y_1 + c_2 \right) + \varepsilon_2 \qquad (2.5)$$

The error ε_1 is assumed uniformly distributed between bounds ε_{1L} and ε_{1H} and analogously for error ε_2. We can interpret these errors in different ways. In particular, where ε_1 has higher variance, the input task will be particularly hard to monitor. Examples would include the task of quality control, or of impact assessment as part of the process of preparing aid proposals. Where ε_2 has higher variance, it is the output task that is particularly hard to monitor, such as the exercise of judgement in evaluating the significance of evidence collected through a routine procedure. An example would be the task of solving a crime: the input task is the comparatively routine task of interviewing witnesses and suspects, while the output task involves deciding which of the suspects is most likely to be guilty. In the context of aid agencies, the input task might be the collection of data about the financial performance of a project; the output task might be the exercise of judgement about whether these data really capture the most important of the project's effects.

As there is no risk aversion in the model, the significance of the uncertainty about output is twofold. Firstly, it reduces the likelihood that a given level of effort on the part of the agent will attain a particular level of any given task; it may therefore blunt incentives for effort. Secondly, it makes any given selection rule on the part of the principal less capable of discriminating between agents of different talents. The impact of this is somewhat subtle, as will be seen below.

There are two periods, 1 and 2. In each period the principal chooses an assignment of tasks to agents. In keeping with the literature on bureaucratic organisations, it is assumed that in the second period the principal has no discretion to offer direct monetary rewards to the agent. Instead the agent is motivated by career concerns – that is, by the wish to demonstrate his talent to the market, which may consist of an internal labour market (such as within the EC or a national bureaucracy). The generosity with which the market rewards observed talent makes a major difference to the structure of incentives within the organisation.

Decisions in period 1 are taken bearing in mind their likely impact on behaviour in period 2, so it is important to work out their effects in period 2 first. The order of events in period 2 is as follows. First the agent decides whether to separate or to bundle the tasks. If the tasks are separated, the principal decides what proportion of the agents to allocate to each task. Then the agents choose their effort levels, and the tasks are carried out.

In period 1 the principal has an additional decision to make. As well as assigning tasks to agents the principal can also choose a promotion rule in the form of a threshold level of performance for each task, above which agents will be selected for employment in period two. As will be seen, this possibility affects the assignment of agents to tasks: there will be an additional bias towards the task, which is easier to monitor because the 'output' of this task now includes information that will improve performance in period 2.

The technical details of the model's results, as well as the formal proofs, are explained in Seabright (1998); a further discussion of implications is in Seabright (2000). The main results are as follows:

(a) In the second period, it will be better for the principal to separate tasks if the output task is relatively hard to monitor, and if the skills required for the two tasks are not strongly positively correlated between agents.[12] Separation will also be better if the input task makes the output task more difficult (such as when the input task involves screening).[13] The principal will tend to prefer bundling them if the output task is relatively easy to monitor, and if there is a strong positive correlation between the skills required for the two tasks.

(b) The principal will allocate agents between tasks in period 2 in order to equalise the marginal returns from the tasks.

---

[12] This supports the reasoning in paragraph 9.4.16 of the Report of the Committee of Independent Experts (1999) where it is stated that '*A priori* control and internal auditing are activities which employ completely different techniques and address completely different concerns. The arrangement whereby they have been kept together within the same directorate-general should be reviewed'.

[13] The result in this special case is consistent with an earlier result due to Dewatripont and Tirole (1997).

(c) Agents' effort on either task in period 1 is lowered if the tasks are hard to monitor, whether the tasks are separated or bundled. In other words, monitoring difficulties blunt work incentives.

(d) Differences in ease of monitoring make no difference to the promotion rules in period 1. Promotion thresholds are chosen so that the same proportion of agents will be promoted from each task.

(e) Separation of tasks is more likely in period 1 than in period 2, all other parameters remaining the same between the two periods. This is because separation yields more information about agents' skills, information that is particularly valuable in period 1 because it improves selection.

(f) Under separation, a higher proportion of agents than in period 2 will be assigned to the low-variance task, both because effort is higher on the low-variance task and because the low-variance task is a more effective screening mechanism. This implies that more of the organisation's resources will be devoted to input-related activities.

These results have some striking implications for the allocation of tasks within an aid agency. They show that, to the extent that the skills appropriate to undertaking the different tasks of an agency tend to be correlated across individuals, these different tasks will tend to be bundled together even though it is known that this will tend to distort incentives towards an undesirable degree of focus on inputs and other routine activities. Financial appraisals will attract more attention than overall impact assessments, for example. Ensuring budgets are spent will take precedence over ensuring they are spent well. There will be a strong bias towards inputs that are easy to monitor rather than outputs that are not. Although, perhaps surprisingly, the promotion rules of an organisation will not be such as to set easier thresholds for those performing easily monitored tasks, they will direct more of the agency's staff towards undertaking those tasks.

What can we conclude? In a set-up like this one, we have seen that uncertainty (the difficulty of monitoring agents' performance) has an important effect on their incentives to exert effort, is irrelevant to determining the necessary rigour of a promotion rule, and significantly affects the allocation of agents to tasks. We should

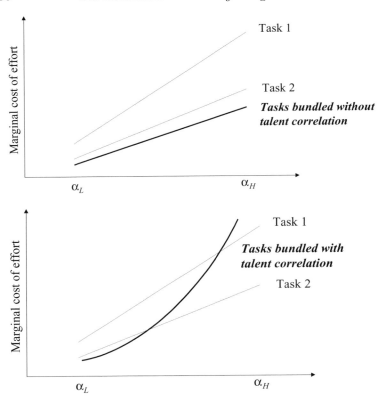

Figure 2.1. The link between talent and effort.

expect a bureaucracy that takes these lessons to heart to allocate more of its members to input- than to output-related tasks, and more of them to routine activities than to those involving judgement and discretion. Likewise, its members themselves are likely to work harder at these input-related activities than at those where their performance, however intrinsically laudable, may fail to find an appreciative audience.

Figure 2.1 shows the intuition behind the first result. It shows effort as a function of talent, both when tasks are separated (thin lines) and when they are bundled (thick line). When talents are uncorrelated, effort is a linear function of talent, but when they

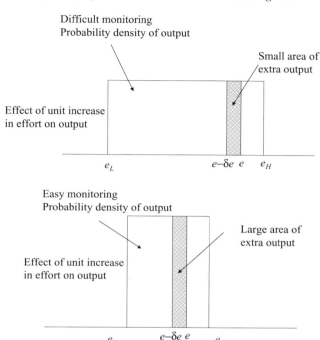

Figure 2.2. The importance of uncertainty for effort – difficult and easy monitoring.

are correlated it is convex. The convexity means that the expected effort levels under bundling may be higher than under separation.

Figure 2.2 shows the intuition behind the third result. Consider a small increase in effort, from a to $a + \delta a$ (we ignore the i subscripts for notational convenience). This means that the threshold value of the error above which the agent is promoted will fall from e to $e - \delta e$. The higher the variance of the error term, the less difference this will make to the probability of promotion. Thus the higher the error variance, the smaller the contribution of any given increase in effort to the probability that the agent will be promoted.

Figures 2.3 and 2.4 demonstrate the intuition behind the last three results. Figure 2.3 shows the unconditional density of talent α_i (again, we suppress i subscripts for convenience), and the subset

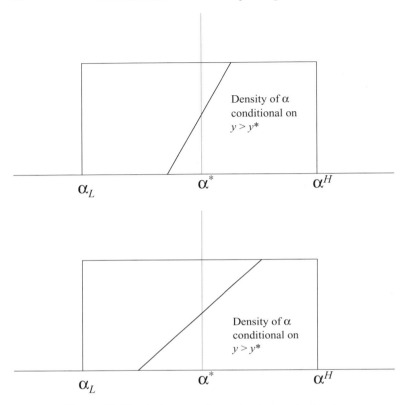

Figure 2.3. The irrelevance of uncertainty for selection 1.

of that density conditional on output lying above some level y which would be produced by an agent of expected talent α. This conditional density has a shape that evidently depends on the magnitude of the error variance. Figure 2.4 shows the impact of two promotion rules a and b with expected talent cut-offs α_a^* and α_b, and subject to different error variances. Suppose these lie at different levels, with $\alpha_b^* > \alpha_a^*$. Then consider a reduction in α_b^*, exactly compensated by an increase in α_a^*, so that the total numbers promoted remain constant. Then the probability mass of those promoted under a falls by exactly the same amount as the probability mass of those promoted under b increases (the boundary

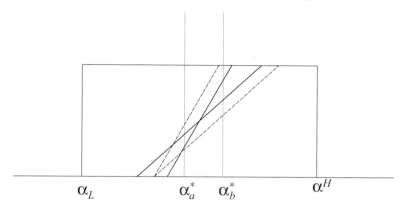

Figure 2.4. The irrelevance of uncertainty for selection 2.

shifts from the broken to the unbroken line in each case). This means that the increase in the expected talent of those promoted under b increases by more than the fall in the expected talent of those promoted under a since the mean talent of the marginal probability mass is lower for a than for b. Therefore equalising the two thresholds from an initial inequality will always strictly increase the expected talent of those promoted. This holds true regardless of the error variances attached to the two promotion rules. Only if $\alpha_a^* = \alpha_b^*$ will the best expected talents be promoted.

However, the diagram also indicates that the expected value of talent conditional on the selection rule α^* is indeed decreasing in the error variance. This means that low-variance tasks when used as screening mechanisms, yield an output of promoted agents with higher expected talent than do high-variance tasks. So the allocation to the tasks will be distorted away from that which equalises the expected return to the two tasks by an amount reflecting the additional value of the low-variance as a screening mechanism.

It is now time to draw together the threads of the argument and to assess conclusions for aid agency organisational design.

5. CONCLUSIONS

Empirical studies of bureaucracy have often failed to distinguish between those aspects of bureaucratic behaviour that reflect poor organisational design and those that are unavoidable consequences of the kind of activity the organisation is obliged to undertake. Some features of organisations, although perhaps regrettable by comparison with an ideal world in which incentives would be unnecessary, are the inevitable result of the fact that individuals' behaviour cannot be precisely monitored. This paper has shown that a degree of input bias, and excessive emphasis on routine activities at the expense of those requiring judgement and discretion, is unavoidable in any organisation where different activities have to be performed but where there is a link between the talents required for different tasks. Separating the input tasks from the output tasks, and the routine tasks from those requiring judgement, would be too costly in terms of failing to exploit the links between these skills. Bundling the tasks together may be the lesser of two evils even though it inevitably leads to a misallocation of agents' efforts towards the inputs.

However, the paper has also shown some of the parameters that will determine the nature of this trade-off. Bad organisational design may get the balance wrong, and an awareness of the factors of importance may be of value in helping to escape the more avoidable shortcomings of bureaucracy.

So what lessons could be learned by aid agencies from the arguments in this paper? Firstly, let us consider the general arguments from the principal–agent literature. Aid agencies that are also public administrations will inevitably suffer from weak organisational incentives due to the particular difficulties of monitoring the results of the work they perform. These will be exacerbated by the absence of direct feedback from beneficiaries to the control mechanisms of the organisation. However, mechanisms to strengthen this feedback will be valuable. Both donor and recipient governments are themselves agents on behalf of their taxpayer-citizens, and should not always be presumed to have the interests of these taxpayer-citizens directly at heart. Once again, mechanisms to strengthen the accountability of aid agencies to these taxpayer-citizens will be valuable (for instance by incorporating non-governmental organisation (NGO) feedback in recipient countries as well as feedback from governments).[14] The activities of aid agencies will tend to

---

[14] Nevertheless, it should not be assumed that all NGOs necessarily represent citizens' true interests either.

concentrate more on input-related tasks (budgets, contracts, personnel) than on output-related tasks where 'success' is relatively difficult to demonstrate. This inputs-bias may be further exacerbated by some of the phenomena to be summarised below.

The main lessons from the literature on multiple principals would seem to be the following. Firstly, being answerable to a number of different constituencies will inevitably lead to some inconsistencies. The fact that sponsors and beneficiaries are not the same will make it difficult to give adequate weight to beneficiaries' interests. Specifically it will reinforce input-bias because donors benefit principally from inputs while beneficiaries benefit mainly from outputs. The presence of such difficulties should not be a cause of despair but should be seen as a challenge to minimise the problems they cause, and in particular to find ways to represent the interests of beneficiaries in the decision-making processes of the agency.

Secondly, the presence of multiple principals can also be a source of strength, provided it enables the agency to commit itself to procedures that would not be easy to implement for a bilateral donor. These include transparent and competitive procedures for tendering and procurement, and a commitment to avoid linking aid to narrow considerations of market access or the fortunes of particular political and economic interest groups. However, this commitment may be easier to deliver on the side of input procedures (tendering and contracting) than on the side of the preparation and selection of projects. This latter fact further reinforces the input bias already described. Mechanisms to mitigate it include more effective delegation of day-to-day aid management from the interests of donors, while keeping donor scrutiny of more long-term strategic aspects of the agency's activities. The creation of Europe Aid, as a predecessor to a specialised agency of the EC, can be seen as a step in this direction, though arguably only a partial step.

Thirdly, multilateralism can also enable the exploitation of economies of scale and scope that are beyond the capacity of bilateral donors. This means that such agencies have a comparative advantage in the implementation of projects and programmes that either require substantial technical expertise, or involve spillover effects between countries or sectors that bilateralism might have difficulty internalising. However, the large scale necessary to cope with such projects will also bring foreseeable inflexibilities, such as a relatively high dependence on seniority systems.

These lessons are not just pious injunctions, for they indicate that a multilateral agency that fails to exploit the benefits that come from the presence of multiple principals is actually likely to perform worse than would bilateral donors. If it cannot find ways to do so it cannot really justify its existence. In particular, transparency of decision-making is an even more important requirement for multilateral agencies than for bilateral ones.[15]

What about lessons from the model of the paper? The main ones are the following. Firstly, an agency will inevitably suffer from a degree of excessive focus upon routine activities; this is likely to include inputs bias, the selection of projects for ease of monitoring rather than overall contribution to beneficiary welfare, a personnel policy that recruits and directs staff to easily monitored tasks, and promotion rules that rely upon performance in these tasks even for selecting people for tasks that require more judgement.

Secondly, it is essential that an agency structure its activities so that it does not suffer from these behavioural characteristics more than is strictly necessary. This means, for example, bundling tasks together only if there is a significant correlation between the skills they require and not merely for administrative convenience. For example, unless financial evaluation of projects involves highly similar skills to those required for overall impact assessment, it is desirable to assign these tasks to different sub-units of the agency (the same argument applies to *ex ante* and *ex post* evaluations). Similarly, tasks involving searching for projects should not be performed by the same units responsible for quality screening of those same projects. Project selection and project auditing should be the responsibility of different units.

Thirdly, separation of tasks is even more important for relatively junior members of an agency, because of the greater information about their skills that such separation yields. Too much generalism among junior staff makes it harder to allocate them subsequently to responsible positions in the organisation.

---

[15] A lesson, incidentally, that does not appear to have been appreciated by the European Central Bank.

To be sure, this is a rich field, which has only recently come to be explored using the tools of incentive theory. There remain many important questions for future work to explore. Nevertheless, one general message remains very clear. Input bias, and a focus on routine tasks at the expense of those requiring discretion and judgement, are here to stay. But their prevalence can be restrained, and the tools of incentive theory provide a number of useful rules of thumb to enable such restraint to be exercised.

REFERENCES

Anderlini, L. (1990) *Manager-Managed Firms.* Mimeo. Cambridge: University of Cambridge.

Armstrong, M., S. Cowan and J. Vickers (1994) *Regulatory Reform: Economic Analysis and British Experience.* Cambridge, Mass.; London: MIT Press.

Bernheim, D. and Whinston, M. (1986) Common Agency. *Econometrica,* 54(4), 923–42.

Browne, S. (1990) *Foreign Aid in Practice.* London: Pinter.

Cassen, R. *et al.* (1994) *Does Aid Work?* Oxford: Clarendon Press.

Chambers, R. (1983) *Rural Development: Putting the Last First.* Harlow: Longman.

Committee of Independent Experts, (1999) *First Report on Allegations regarding Fraud, Mismanagement and Nepotism in the European Commission.* Brussels: European Commission.

De Waal, A. (1998) *Famine Crimes: Politics and the Disaster Relief Industry in Africa.* Bloomington, Indiana: Indiana University Press.

Dewatripont, M. *et al.* (2000) *Missions and Accountability of Government Agencies.* Mimeo. Toulouse: IDEI.

Downs, A. (1967) *Inside Bureaucracy.* Rand Corporation research study. Boston, MA: Little and Brown.

Holmstrom, B. (1982) Managerial incentive problems: a dynamic perspective. In *Essays in Economics and Management in Honor of Lars Wahlbeck.* Helsinki: Swedish School of Economics.

Holmstrom, B. and P. Milgrom (1991) Multi-task principal–agent analyses: incentive contracts, asset ownership and job design. *Journal of Law, Economics and Organization,* 7, 24–52.

Kapur, D. *et al.* (1997) *The World Bank: Its First Half Century.* Washington, D.C., The Brookings Institution.

Lake, A. (1989) *Somoza Falling.* Amherst: University of Massachusetts Press.

Lal, D. (1983) *The Poverty of Development Economics.* London: Institute of Economic Affairs.

Lele, U. (1990) *Aid to African Agriculture: Lessons from Two Decades of Donor Experience.* Washington, DC: The World Bank.

Lipton, M. and J. Toye (1990) *Does Aid Work In India?* London: Routledge.

Martimort, D. (1993) *Multi-Principals as a Commitment Mechanism.* Mimeo. University of Toulouse.

Mason, E. and R. Asher (1973) *The World Bank Since Bretton Woods.* Washington, DC: The Brookings Institution.

Mookherjee, D. (1984): Optional Incentive Schemes with Many Agents. *Review of Economic Studies,* 51(3), 433–446.

Mosley, P., Harrigan, J., and Toye, J. (1991) *Aid and Power: the World Bank and Policy-Based Lending.* London: Routledge.

Neven, D., P. Papandropoulos and P. Seabright (1998) *Trawling for Minnows: European Competition Policy and Agreements Between Firms.* London: Centre for Economic Policy Research.

Satyanarayan, S. (2000) *Displacement and Compensation in Large Dam Projects.* Ph.D. dissertation: University of Cambridge.

Seabright, P. (1998) *Multiple Talents for Multiple Tasks.* Mimeo. University of Cambridge.

Seabright, P. (2000) Skill versus judgment and the architecture of organizations. *European Economic Review,* 44(4–6), 856–868.

3

The interactions of donors, contractors, and recipients in implementing aid for institutional reform

Peter Murrell

1. THE GENERAL CONTEXT

The efficiency of the mechanisms of foreign aid provision has rarely been the subject of analytical deliberation (Pietrobelli and Scarpa, 1992). This lacuna is mirrored in the real world of foreign aid provision. The byzantine bureaucratic structure of aid agencies, the weak economic incentives in aid contracts, and the imprecision of project evaluation seem inconsistent with the pursuit of economic efficiency in this vital, and very large, area of economic activity. To cite one example, there are no existing evaluation methods suitable for application to the dominant types of aid projects in the Tacis and Phare programs, institutional reform projects (Evaluation Unit, 1997a, p.7; Martens, 1998).

The purpose of this chapter is to use some elementary economic analysis to understand the contractual and organisational determinants of the efficiency of foreign aid provision. The chapter focuses on institutional reform projects, both because these are becoming increasingly common and because the difficulties in organising foreign aid provision are particularly acute for such projects. This introduction examines why there has been little analysis of the efficiency of foreign aid mechanisms in the past, why economic analysis has much to offer in this sphere, and why changing views of the role of government make this an especially propitious juncture to apply economic analysis. This introduction ends with a road map to the remainder of the chapter.

The author gratefully acknowledges support for this study from the European Commission's Tacis programme and from the IRIS Center of the University of Maryland.

The reasons for the lack of academic study of the mechanisms of foreign aid provision are both general and specific. As Tirole (1994, p.1) remarks, the internal organization of government is a subject that has received relatively limited attention from theoretical economists. Indeed, the formal analysis of bureaucratic organisations is still in a very underdeveloped state (Seabright, 2000). Intrinsic properties of government activities – multiple goals, problems in using high-powered incentives in the presence of large externalities, difficulties in ascertaining the relationship between actions and outcomes – make the study of government organisation a particularly challenging exercise, especially for the economics discipline, which places great weight on deriving results from analytical models. Yet it is economists, rather than other social scientists, who have a peculiar concern for efficiency.

These problematic aspects of government activities are writ large in foreign aid processes, especially within aid projects that involve institutional reform, which are now high on the list of donor priorities.[1] Two governments (and often multilateral donors) have a stake in outcomes, multiplying objectives. Externalities are intrinsic in the functioning of institutions. Success in implementing projects will often require taking into account local idiosyncrasies, or embeddedness (Granovetter, 1985). When embeddedness is present, donor agencies will have only cursory knowledge of the relationship between actions and outcomes. Therefore, the involvement of recipients will be necessary if the project is to be a success. But this means that donor control of project activities is made more difficult.

These features of aid projects also suggest the baleful effect of interest groups. Institutional reform is an attempt to change the very basic rules of an economy. It is natural that powerful political groups, and the governmental bureaucracy itself, will care deeply about outcomes. With two governments involved and two sets of interest groups, the political economy of aid multiplies in complexity. With recipient-country agencies having an integral role, interest groups have another entré to parlay their influence. As is shown in later sections of this chapter, when there is the simultaneous

[1] See Mummert, Chapter 4, for a detailed discussion of the nature of institutional reform.

possibility of embeddedness and interest group activity, the informational picture is even more clouded than usual.

However, a confluence of several factors makes the present juncture an appropriate moment to focus more explicitly on analysis of the efficiency of foreign aid processes. There have been great advances since the 1980s in the economic theory of organisation with the systematisation of the three main paradigms of informational economics, adverse selection, moral hazard, and incomplete contracting (Tirole, 1994). There is a burgeoning literature that extends this theory beyond the domain of profit-maximising entities.[2] Moreover, in the area of institutional reform, significant advances are being made in understanding how institutions work and in ascertaining the relationships between institutional inputs and economic outcomes.[3]

On the practical front, the experiences provided by the privatisation, deregulation, and the re-focusing of government that occurred in the 1980s and 1990s have enhanced the perception that there are large efficiency gains to be derived from using economic analysis to inform government operations. There has been a dramatic shift in the *Weltanschauung* of the role of government. A former view held an ideological or sectoral conception of the domain of the public sector, associating that sector with government supply and government production. Now, there is increasing acceptance of the view that the role of government should reflect pragmatic concerns, focusing on what government can and cannot do in the light of the specific informational and incentive problems that arise in different areas of economic activity.[4]

At this juncture, then, the new theoretical developments can combine with an increasingly pragmatic approach to the role of government to suggest that much can be gained by analysing the mechanisms of foreign aid provision. An essential element of this analysis is the application of existing theoretical tools and results

---

[2] Laffont and Tirole (1993), for example, present a large number of insights into regulation and the organisation of government. Hart *et al.* (1997) provide a systematic analysis of which activities should remain in government and which should be reserved for the private sector. For further examples, see Shapiro and Willig (1990) and Schmidt (1996).

[3] See, for example, the collection of papers in Clague (1997) and the citations found therein.

[4] Even within the community of economists the former view held sway through the 1970s. The modern theory of organisation has done much to loosen the hold.

to the specific features of foreign aid. Such applied economics can offer practical guidelines for the design and evaluation of aid projects by clarifying the consequences of different forms of project organisation and by suggesting cogent evaluation criteria. This paper's applied economic theory is cast in such a vein.

The approach taken in this chapter follows from two characteristics that are inherent in institutional-reform aid projects. These are discussed more fully in Section 2. Firstly, the output produced by such projects is a public good whose quality varies in not-easily-ascertainable ways. Therefore, adverse selection, moral hazard, and incomplete contracts are bound to be at the centre of any exercise that models the production of institutional reform. Secondly, there is the multiplicity of actors and interactions within aid projects. There are two political-bureaucratic systems (those of donor and recipient countries). Moreover, projects usually rely on the expertise of an independent contractor, who must work closely with both donor and recipient agencies, but does so in a self-seeking manner.[5]

This chapter particularly focuses on the problems arising from the presence of an intermediary contractor, hired by the donor to help implement an institutional reform. Section 3 builds a tractable model of the interactions between donor, contractor, and recipient. The model admits comparative statics exercises that provide an understanding of the effects of different types of project implementation arrangements. For example, the model provides answers to the following questions: What is the effect of delegating control of the project to the aid recipient? How are project outcomes affected by changes in the quality of information produced by monitoring and evaluation? What is the effect of different types of private (profit, not-for-profit) contractors?

Section 4 derives the equilibria that occur under varying contractual arrangements. Section 5 analyses the properties of each of the model's equilibria under differing assumptions about the nature of the project being implemented and the severity of principal–agent problems in the recipient country. Section 6 adds some further comparative statics, providing examples that suggest the

---

[5] Putzel (1998) emphasizes the importance of the independent contractor in every phase of European Union aid projects.

flexibility of the model in understanding the effects of perturbations of the contracting environment. Section 7 suggests ways in which contract design and evaluation can help the donor counteract the deleterious influence of interest groups and to take into account the embeddedness properties of institutional reforms. Section 8 establishes the empirical relevance of the model by using it to interpret the facts of three real-world examples of aid projects. This section shows how the model's analysis can help in interpreting the underlying causes of success and failure in aid projects. Section 9 concludes with a summary of the lessons derived from the model.

2. SETTING THE STAGE FOR A MODEL: AN OVERVIEW OF INSTITUTIONAL REFORM PROJECTS

The product

The nature of the product created during institutional reform lies at the heart of the special difficulties in organising efficient projects (Evaluation Unit, 1997a, pp. 15–16). Institutional reform is a public good: non-excludability means that market mechanisms cannot be used to secure an accurate measure of willingness to pay. Although methods to finesse this problem have been developed in recent years, particularly within environmental economics, the characteristics of institutional reform make implementation of these methods particularly difficult. There are often extremely large numbers of actors who benefit. (Consider improvements in contract law.) Moreover, because some institutions simply coordinate expectations and establish credibility, the benefit provided by an institution cannot be inferred from observations of active use.[6] In some instances (e.g. a credible court system), the most effective institutions might be used the least. Thus, it will usually be impossible to obtain an estimate of the ultimate benefit of institutional reform. As a consequence, project design, contractual stipulations, and project evaluation will focus on some intermediate output, for example, the passage of a law or the training of a bureaucracy.[7]

---

[6] In some cases, for example standards, use is extremely difficult to observe.

[7] This paragraph highlights only the small subset of features of institutional reform that are pertinent to the development of the model. To be sure, institutional reform presents many more difficulties than the ones noted here, as Mummert, Chapter 4, clearly shows.

The fact that institutions are embedded in their socio-economic environment now becomes important. At its simplest level, embeddedness implies that the optimal institutional reform varies with subtle characteristics of the socio-economic environment (Granovetter, 1985). Moreover, there are widely divergent theories and empirical evidence on the effectiveness of different institutional forms in different contexts (North, 1990). These observations have two implications. Firstly, even when an intermediate institutional output, such as a law, is perfectly observable, the project supervisor in a development agency cannot know whether that output has been produced in the right quantity, or with the correct parameters, or at the appropriate quality, for the socio-economic environment in question. This would require too deep a knowledge of the recipient-country environment for any remote bureaucracy in Brussels or in Washington. Secondly, perfect observability is not likely. Subtle variations in *de facto* institutional form are not obvious to an outside observer who only perceives the *de jure* institution. The scope for moral hazard in project implementation is immense.

The above implies that important project implementation decisions will be in the hands of implementers, those working on the ground. The decisions cannot be contracted, because of imperfect information. They also cannot be second-guessed during evaluation, or at least during any evaluation that is not based on knowledge that is as intimate as that of the implementers. Indeed, as cosmetic but essential variations in institutions (e.g. the terminology used in a law) are difficult for an outsider to distinguish from substantive changes, it must be assumed that an outsider only observes a very crude indicator of project implementation. Incomplete contracts are the norm.

A final, and crucial, feature of institutional reform projects derives from their political prominence. Such projects affect large numbers of actors in important ways and they are therefore likely to be the object of intense political focus. Interest groups will care greatly about the details of project implementation. These interests will be particularly difficult to understand for outsiders who are unfamiliar with the arcane features of the political economy of a recipient country. Hence, institutional reform projects are likely to be particularly prone to the distorting effects of interest group pressures.

The actors

Who are the actors in an institutional reform aid project? Let us take a typical Tacis project as the archetype.[8] These projects involve:

- the European Commission (EC) and the EC delegation, acting implicitly on behalf of the political bodies of the European Union (EU), and ultimately the voters in the member states
- the Coordinating Unit within the Newly Independent States (NIS), acting implicitly on behalf of the political bodies of that state and ultimately its citizens
- the task manager, who is a staff member of the EC responsible for administering a number of aid contracts
- a contractor hired to implement the project
- a project partner, an organisation within the NIS that implements the project and is usually the direct recipient of the assistance in the sense that the project partner has most interest in implementation.

The nature of the links between these entities significantly influences the ways in which projects are implemented. The task manager is under the formal authority of the EC institutions in a principal–agent relationship. The project partner is usually subject to the NIS government, providing another principal–agent relationship.[9] The project partner and the task manager are linked in a quasi-contractual arrangement (a statement of endorsement). There is a formal contract between the contractor and the EC, administered by the task manager.

---

[8] See Evaluation Unit, 1997b, p.2 'Tacis Objectives and Programme Description'. The organisation of Phare activities is similar in structure, but with more authority and implementation tasks in the hands of the Programme Management Unit, which is set up by the recipient country (Evaluation Unit 1997a, pp.20–21).

[9] In some cases, the connection is tight, as when the project partner is a governmental department. In other cases, the link is less formal, as when a non-governmental organisation is implementing a project. But in all aid projects, the recipient government exerts much influence over the choice of project partner and whether that partner benefits from future aid projects. Therefore the project partner can be viewed as a subordinate.

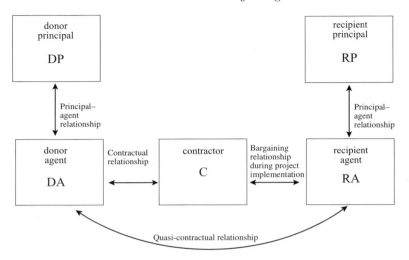

Figure 3.1. The actors and their relationships.

The only formal link between contractor and project partner is that they are thrust together in the same project. Given that each has its own interests in the project and given that the informational properties of institutional reform projects rule out complete contracts, there is much scope for bargaining between contractor and project partner.

Although the names of the participants may vary, this form of organization is typical for development projects. In the United States Agency for International Development (US AID), it is absolutely standard. In multilateral organisations, such as the World Bank, the arrangement is similar, although the contractor is quite often an in-house department.[10] A generic structure of interactions therefore falls into place for modelling purposes. This generic structure is depicted in Figure 3.1. The actors to be taken into account in modelling aid implementation are:

- The donor principal (DP), which sometimes might be narrowly interpreted as the immediate bureaucratic superiors of the donor

[10] In the latest incarnation of the World Bank's organisational structure, the in-house contractor has an internal-market type interaction with the department in charge of project formulation.

aid agency or more broadly interpreted as political leaders, or the citizens of the donor country (Seabright, Chapter 2);

- The donor agent (DA), the specific bureaucracy in the donor country that administers the details of the aid program (e.g. the Tacis or Phare bureaucracy or US AID);[11]
- The contractor (C), appearing in different incarnations depending on the way in which the project is implemented. The most typical examples are a for-profit consultancy, a not-for-profit organisation, or a non-governmental-organisation (NGO) from the donor country. In special cases, the contractor might be interpreted as a separate arm of the governmental bureaucracy of the donor country, where specialised project implementation has been contracted in-house (as when the US Treasury department implements tax reform projects for US AID). The contractor and the donor agent will have a contractual relationship, one that is enforceable in donor country courts, to the extent that any incomplete contract is;
- The recipient principal (RP), narrowly interpreted as the immediate bureaucratic superiors of the recipient-country organisation implementing the aid project or more broadly interpreted as the political leaders, or even the citizens of the recipient country;
- The recipient agent (RA), the specific organisation in the recipient country that undertakes detailed implementation of the reform project. This organisation could be an element of the recipient country's bureaucracy (as in the case of legal reform, for example) or a private organisation (for example, an NGO or a start-up business advisory service), which nevertheless is effectively subordinate to the recipient government given that government's influence over the disbursal of aid funds. The recipient agent and the donor agent will have a formal, perhaps contractual, relationship, but this will not be enforceable in any court. Enforcement mechanisms will usually rely on the relationship between donor and recipient principals or on an ongoing relationship between the donor agent and the recipient agent.

[11] In this chapter, the distinction between the donor agent and the donor principal is not emphasised, in order to make the analysis tractable. In reality, of course, this distinction is immensely important, as Seabright, Chapter 2, makes clear.

The above provides an overview. The next section fills out the picture by making more precise assumptions in order to model the determination of project outcomes.

3. MODELLING THE INTERACTIONS BETWEEN AID RECIPIENTS

The model's focus is on the effect of the independent contractor, who is under contract to the donor agent and in a bargaining relationship with the recipient agent. The model pinpoints the consequences of the contractor's flexibility. This is a consequence of the donor's imperfect information on implementation and can be used to the contractor's advantage because of the recipient agent's desire to distort project outcomes. It also examines the consequences of different types of relationships between the contractor and the recipient agent, which vary according to the specifications of the contracts between the donor and the contractor and according to the nature of the prior relationship between the contractor and the recipient agent.

Definitions and assumptions

The basic elements of the model follow the analysis developed by Shleifer and Vishny (1994), whose underlying structure rests on the incomplete contracts model of Grossman and Hart (1986) and Hart and Moore (1990). The Shleifer and Vishny (1994) analysis examines the effects of government ownership and privatisation. Their context and the present one – privatisation and aid projects – are very different in their surface phenomena, but similar attributes underlie each. Incomplete contracts reflect incomplete information; the locus of control affects the nature of decisions; and informal bargaining results from incomplete contracts.

The contractor is an independent entity maximising profits. The contractor is charged with facilitating project implementation, using the expertise that it possesses, which is unavailable in both recipient and donor bureaucracies.[12] The contractor is hired to

---

[12] For example, the administrators in charge of the Polish standards harmonisation process did not have sufficient information concerning what was required and the foreign expertise that was necessary (Klugt *et al*, p.50).

draft a law that is as close as possible to western standards and that will be passed in the recipient country. Therefore, one specific interpretation of the model to be used in this paper is a project in which a potential EU member is acquiring the *Acquis Communitaire*, the set of laws that must be adopted to qualify for membership. While the contractor and the recipient agent can acquire enough information to know how the law will work in practice, the donor principal and the donor agent do not have the resources for such exact observation.[13] The donor principal and the donor agent can observe *de jure* law, the formal statute on the books. But *de facto* law might be quite different in both substance and effect from what one would predict with only the knowledge of *de jure* law. Thus, the contract between the donor agent and the contractor can condition payment only on passage of the *de jure* law. This informational and contractual structure is a natural consequence of the embeddedness assumption: those not working on the ground have little grasp of the subtleties apparent to those enmeshed in the details of a society's arrangements.[14]

The observability assumptions lead to a particularly concise modeling of project outcomes. Assume that the law has some measurable dimension, captured in the variable L.[15] L is a property of the *de facto* law, one element of which is whether any law has been implemented – whether a *de jure* law is on the statute books. A value $L \leq 0$ for the *de facto* law signifies that the *de jure* law has not been implemented, since no *de facto* law exists if no *de jure* law is on the books. All parties have sufficient observational capabilities to differentiate between the cases of non-implementation ($L \leq 0$)

[13] Moreover, neither the contractor nor the recipient agent can provide credible evidence. For example, a study of the approximation process in Poland observes that it is extremely difficult to obtain an accurate insight into the application and enforcement of Polish legislation (Klugt *et al.*, 1997, p.25).

[14] These informational assumptions are most pertinent when the contractor and the donor agent are in a one-time relationship. When the contractor and the donor agent have repeated interactions, trust and reputational effects might mitigate the informational problems. However, the one-shot relationship is rather typical of aid projects, since the employees of donor agencies find themselves frequently moving from country to country and function to function.

[15] In one interpretation, L might be quality. The present model focuses on L as capturing some parameter of the reform, say the amount of training given to enforcement agencies or the efforts to embody prevailing business relationships in the reform or the degree to which this reform is structured to be complementary to other institutions.

and implementation ($L > 0$). But given that the donor agent does not observe *de facto* law, the payment from the donor agent to the contractor can be conditioned only on whether L is positive or not, not on any specific value of L.[16]

The donor would like implementation at $L = L^w$, that is with the new law in the recipient country to be identical to a standard developed country or donor country law. Because keeping in the good graces of Western aid agencies is an important political goal, the recipient principal has decided that it wants to be seen as satisfying donor requirements. Nevertheless, it is possible that the level L^w is not optimal for the recipient principal, even though implementation of L^w will improve the situation over the status quo.

The process of drafting the law is quite technical, but straightforward for the contractor and involves the recipient agent very little. The contractor is most adept at donor-country legal practices and therefore $L = L^w$ is the reform that is easiest for the contractor to accomplish. To produce $L = L^w$, the contractor uses resources that cost K. When the *de jure* law is on the statute books, the contractor receives a payment that the donor agent knows is sufficient to cover the cost of producing the law, that is K.

Given the incomplete contract between the contractor and the donor agent, there is scope for flexibility in project implementation. This flexibility is most crucial in the stage when modifications are made in the law in order to secure adoption by the government and the legislature and in the stage when implementation decisions are made. Formal adoption will require modification in the law to satisfy the requirements of important interest groups. How the law is actually implemented will affect the status and the workload of different organisations and governmental agencies in the recipient country. Administrations might want a law that minimises implementation costs. Moreover, given the embedded nature of law, modifications in the draft might well make the law much more effective in the country.

Thus, deviations in L from L^w alter the net benefit that the recipient agent derives from implementation. Assume that $R(L)$

---

[16] Evaluation Unit (1997a, pp.20–21) suggests that the European Commission does not allocate resources to generate the in-house expertise that would allow for more detailed contractual stipulations. Therefore, Phare programmes have vague definitions of objectives.

measures the benefits of L to the recipient agent, with $R(0) = 0$. Importantly, moving away from L^w in one direction can improve the recipient agent's situation. Assume that $(\partial R(L)/\partial L) = R_L > 0$ and introduce the usual assumption that $R_{LL} < 0$.[17] (Throughout this chapter, partial derivatives are represented by subscripts.) The information that the recipient principal has on L and the preferences of the recipient principal over L are left for later discussion.

The contractor will be subject to pressures to revise its draft law. Given the assumptions already made on observability of L, the contractor can do so without jeopardising payment from the donor, so long as $L > 0$. To adapt the law, the contractor must expend additional resources. Its experts will have to spend additional time in-country co-ordinating with local officials. Local labour will be required for fact gathering and for acquiring the necessary information from the local interest groups and bureaucracies. To model these extra costs, assume that the cost of producing L is $K + k(|L - L^w|)$, for $L > 0$.[18] K and k are common knowledge.

As in many aid projects, the recipient country contributes resources for project implementation.[19] Let S denote the cost to the recipient agent of the recipient resources devoted to the project. $S \geq S^w$ is necessary for project implementation. Assume, as is standard in aid projects, that the recipient principal gives the recipient agent resources, S^w, on agreeing to implement the project.[20] But the recipient agent can supply additional help for project implementation. This help might be especially valuable to the contractor when the institutional reform is an embedded project, which requires local resources both to gain an understanding of complementarities between institutions and to ensure that L matches the socio-economic environment.

---

[17] These assumptions could be relaxed a great deal without affecting the conclusions of the paper. For example, it is purely a matter of convention to assume that $R_L > 0$ at L^w rather than the reverse. Similarly, given that $R_L > 0$ at L^w, it is eminently consistent with the model that as L increases one could encounter a range at which $R_L < 0$.

[18] Linearity is purely a convenience here. A range of assumptions would be consistent with conclusions obtained.

[19] The political credibility of reforms and the co-ordination of reforms in different areas will usually require local input.

[20] But assume that $R(L^w) - S^w > R(0)$, meaning that the recipient agent prefers the Western-style project to nothing, even if it has to expend its own resources on the project. Ultimately, S^w usually comes from aid funds, but ones that have many alternative uses for the recipient principal.

When the recipient agent supplies more than S^w to the project, the task of the contractor is made easier. This can be modelled by assuming that domestic resources in the amount S allow the contractor to save $\theta\phi(S)$ in the costs of producing a reform. ($\theta > 0$ is a shift parameter whose importance will be made clear at a later juncture.) $\phi(S) = 0$ for $S \leqq S^w$, because a law cannot be produced without minimal participation of the recipient agent. For $S \geqq S^w$, $\phi(S)$ conforms to standard assumptions: $\phi_S > 0$, and $\phi_{SS} < 0$. $\phi(.)$ is common knowledge, but only the recipient agent and the contractor know θ. the donor agent and the recipient principal know when $S \leqq S^w$, but cannot observe the exact value of S.[21]

Contractual arrangements

The contract signed between the contractor and the donor agent exchanges K for implementation of the project, while that between the recipient agent and the recipient principal exchanges S^w for implementation. The donor agent and the recipient principal have sufficient information to know whether it is the contractor and the recipient agent who has defaulted on its obligations if the project is not implemented. Thus, when the contractor is deemed responsible for $L \leqq 0$, the contractor forfeits K (and similarly for the recipient agent and S^w).[22]

The equilibrium outcome will depend upon the nature of the interaction between the recipient agent and the contractor, before project implementation begins. There are four plausible scenarios. In cases (i) and (ii) control of the project is not shared. In cases (iii) and (iv), there is shared control of the project. The difference between the two cases centres on whether or not there is bargaining:

(i) The contractor takes effective charge of the project and the recipient agent has no bargaining power. The contractor knows

---

[21] This is a baseline assumption, which can be altered when one introduces monitoring and evaluation.

[22] This assumption serves only to clarify a detail in the contracts signed by the contractor and the recipient agent, which primarily affects the participation constraints of the parties. These assumptions do not affect the qualitative nature of the results.

the recipient agent's trade-off between the output produced (L) by the technical resources that the contractor devotes to the project ($K + k(|L - L^w|)$) and the local help (S) that the recipient agent is willing to contribute. Thus, the contractor will decide upon the level of technical resources that it is willing to devote to the project and inform the recipient agent how much local help would be appropriate given this particular level of technical resources. As the recipient agent has no bargaining power, this is a take it or leave it proposition. Of course, the deal that the contractor offers the recipient agent must meet the recipient agent's participation constraint.

(ii) The recipient agent takes effective charge of the project and the contractor has no bargaining power. The recipient agent knows the contractor's trade-off between the local help that the recipient agent devotes to the project and the technical resources that the contractor is willing to contribute in return. Thus, the recipient agent will announce the amount of local help that it is willing to devote to the project and inform the contractor how much technical assistance will be appropriate given this particular level of local help. As the contractor has no bargaining power, this is a take it or leave it proposition for the contractor and the recipient agent designs the deal so that it just meets the contractor's participation constraint.

(iii) The contractor decides on the level of technical resources it is willing to devote to the project and the recipient agent decides on the level of local help. The contractor and the recipient agent make their own decisions separately without negotiations.

(iv) The contractor decides on the level of technical resources it is willing to devote to the project and the recipient agent decides on the level of local help. The contractor and the recipient agent negotiate and bargain to a mutually advantageous outcome.

Each of these arrangements is plausible and has arisen frequently in aid projects. For example, in Tacis projects, it appears that arrangement (i) is the most usual, perhaps because project partners are involved late in the process and are forced to accept existing decisions: 'the project partners are not sufficiently involved in the formulation of the [terms of agreement] and have very little rights vis-a-vis the contractor in the management of the project.'[23] Similarly in Phare programmes, 'the contractor's informational advantage allowed them to drive the future course of action . . .' (Evaluation Unit 1997a, p.21). Arrangement (i) is also common in US AID projects due to the contractor's informal advantage and its closeness to US AID.[24]

However, in recent years, recipient 'ownership' of a project has been emphasised by donors, where ownership has come to mean that the recipient agent has a significant influence over project decisions. The ultimate in ownership is arrangement (ii). If a desire for recipient ownership is combined with a situation where it is essential for the contractor to have authority over its own expertise, then (iii) and (iv) are the natural outcomes. These are the most likely arrangements for Phare in the future, where accession-driven objectives will determine the content of the programs but the desire for decentralisation leads to an emphasis on the role of recipient bureaucracy in implementation (Evaluation Unit,1997a, pp.17–21).

As project outcomes depend critically on which of the four arrangements is chosen, it is important to examine the factors that determine this choice. Here, a few suggestions can be made. Firstly, as is apparent from the Tacis, Phare and US AID examples above, the donor bureaucracy's process of project generation is crucial: if the recipient is left in the dark until implementation, then control is likely to be held by the contractor. This is also the case when contractors bring projects to the attention of the donor agent: they often have in mind compliant recipient agents.[25] Secondly, when the recipient country has political power the recipient agent will likely have greater control. A powerful agency in a reforming country can sometimes choose between many contractors and will therefore have influence over the specification of the contract. Thirdly, the degree of sophistication in institutional reform in the recipient country is important, an example being the passive role of

---

[23] See the 'Project Cycle Management and Tacis Staffing' Chapter of Evaluation Unit (1997b, p.2).

[24] This comment is based on the author's own personal observations of many US AID projects.

[25] These processes of contractor control are discussed in Putzel (1998).

recipients in many Central Asian projects in contrast to the active role in Central Europe. Lastly, donor experience matters. Where the donor is inexperienced and the contractor is knowledgeable, contractor control is likely. In contrast, an experienced donor can find a recipient agent who can use 'ownership' productively.

4. THE FOUR EQUILIBRIA

During project implementation, participants choose the level of technical assistance contributed by the contractor and the level of local help contributed by the recipient agent. The level of L is a product of these decisions. The aim of the aid project is the creation of L and project success or failure is a function of this variable. Thus, the analysis will focus on L. The set up of the model allows us to do this since a specific choice of the contractor's technical assistance immediately translates into a specific value of L.

Figure 3.2 depicts the objectives of the parties and their partic016ipation constraints in the (S, L) plane. The curvature properties of

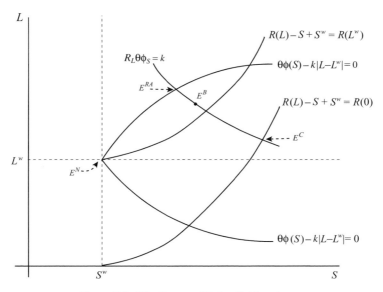

Figure 3.2. The four equilibria of aid projects.

the relationships in that figure follow directly from the assumptions made above. As all project-implementing equilibria fall in the area where $(S, L) \geqq (S^w, L^w)$, the following discussion will focus on that region of the diagram.

During project implementation, the contractor maximises: $K + \theta\phi(S) - (K + k(|L - L^w|)) = \theta\phi(S) - k(|L - L^w|)$. The contractor will participate in the project if $\theta\phi(S) - k(|L - L^w|) \geqq 0$. Figure 3.2 depicts the locus of points that satisfy this constraint with equality: the contractor will not agree to an equilibrium above this locus and prefers equilibria below it.

The recipient agent maximises $R(L) - S + S^w$, while its participation constraint is $R(L) - S + S^w \geqq R(0)$ and $S \geqq S^w$ (because if this latter inequality is not satisfied the project is not implemented). The recipient agent will not agree to an equilibrium below the locus $R(L) - S + S^w = R(0)$ and prefers equilibria above it. $R(L) - S + S^w = R(L^w)$ depicts the recipient agent's indifference curve that passes through (S^w, L^w).

The possibility of moral hazard in project implementation is a necessary condition for a non-trivial problem. Without moral hazard, when there are no gains to be made from moving away from (S^w, L^w), the determination of equilibrium is obvious. There is a natural assumption that rules out this trivial case, ensuring that there are outcomes satisfying both parties' participation constraints other than the one envisaged by the donor, (S^w, L^w), and the no-project point, $(0, 0)$. Such outcomes exist if $\theta\phi_S(S^w)R_L(L^w) > k$.[26] Given this assumption, the locus $\theta\phi_S R_L = k$ plays a central role in the analysis.[27] This locus contains the set of points that would be obtained by maximising the recipient agent's welfare holding the contractor's constant (or vice versa): it is the bargaining set of co-operative game theory (Binmore, 1992, section 5.4). Given the assumptions on the functions that appear above, this locus is downward sloping, which guarantees the uniqueness of equilibrium

---

[26] Consider an incremental move $(\Delta S, \Delta L)$ from (S^w, L^w) that leaves the contractor just as well off as at (S^w, L^w). Then $\theta\phi_S(S^w)\Delta S = k\Delta L$. This move leaves R better off if $R_L(L^w)\Delta L > \Delta S$. This is the case if $\theta\phi_S(S^w)R_L(L^w) > k$.

[27] It is of course a further assumption that the locus, $\theta\phi_S R_L = k$, exists, which will be the case if it is not always in the interests of the contractor and the recipient agent to bargain for ever higher levels of L and S. Sufficient conditions for this to be the case are that $\phi_S \to 0$ as $S \to \infty$ or $R_L \to 0$ as $L \to \infty$.

in each of the pertinent regimes. The ensuing paragraphs examine the characteristics of these equilibria.

E^C: The contractor makes the decisions – the recipient agent has no bargaining power

The contractor chooses the level of technical resources it contributes and the level of local help that it wants the recipient agent to give in return. The contractor wants to maximize $\theta\phi(S) - k(|L - L^w|)$ subject to $R(L) - S + S^w \geqq R(0)$. The equilibrium is in the region $(S, L) > (S^w, L^w)$ and satisfies $\theta\phi_S R_L = k$ and $R(L) - S + S^w = R(0)$. It is labeled E^C in Figure 3.2, the superscript denoting the actor making the decisions. Vesting control in the contractor gives the contractor all rents that accrue from the relationship between contractor and recipient agent.

E^{RA}: The recipient agent makes the decisions – the contractor has no bargaining power

The recipient agent chooses the level of local help it contributes and the technical assistance that it asks the contractor to contribute in return. The recipient agent maximizes $R(L) - S + S^w$ subject to $\theta\phi(S) - k(|L - L^w|) \geqq 0$. The equilibrium conditions are $\theta\phi_S R_L = k$ and $\theta\phi(S) - k(|L - L^w|) = 0$, which are satisfied at E^{RA} in Figure 3.2. Naturally, vesting control in the recipient agent rather than the contractor transfers all rents to the former, but it also has important effects on outcomes. The implemented law is farther from the EU-desired outcome. The recipient agent expends more of its own resources. The implications of these points are examined in the next section after deliberation on the nature of the preferences of the donor principal and the recipient principal.[28]

E^N: Divided control over project decisions – no bargaining

When control is split, two obvious possibilities arise. If the parties are strangers and cannot reach a modicum of co-operation

---

[28] This configuration of the model corresponds most closely to Kanbur and Sandler's (1999) innovative proposals for reform of the development assistance. Therefore, the results developed below reflect on the consequences of implementing their proposals, suggesting how the outputs of projects will change. Kanbur and Sandler rely on competition between recipients and between donors to mitigate the problems identified in this chapter.

or if project implementation decisions are made before the parties are in contact, each makes decisions separately. Then it is reasonable to assume that a Nash equilibrium results. This case seems to be the norm in Tacis projects for example, where the time lag between project identification and implementation is so long that 'when the contractor and project partner finally meet, it is not uncommon to discover that their approaches to project strategy differ considerably.'[29]

Given any level of $S \geqq S^w$, the contractor will choose to devote an amount of technical assistance that leads to $L = L^w$. Given $L = L^w$, the recipient agent will choose $S = S^w$, the minimum level of S that ensures that the project will be implemented. Thus, there is a unique project-implementing Nash equilibrium (S^w, L^w). There is also another Nash equilibrium at $(0,0)$, but this is Pareto-dominated by (L^w, S^w). When implementation decisions are made, the parties have already agreed (with the recipient principal and with the donor agent) to implement the aid project and therefore $(0, 0)$ is effectively ruled out. For these reasons, (S^w, L^w) will be the natural equilibrium when there is no bargaining.

E^B: Divided control over project decisions – no bargaining
Under some circumstances, the parties will be able to bargain to a joint outcome. For example, 'in some [Tacis] projects, the [project partners] or contractors have insisted on . . . 'Joint Project Management' between themselves and this is on record as having had a positive influence on the transparency and co-operation within the project.'[30] Then, assume that the parties negotiate to the Nash bargaining equilibrium (Binmore, 1992, Chapter 5). This will lie on the $\theta \phi_S R_L = k$ locus, its exact location depending upon the bargaining power of the two parties and their threat (or disagreement) points.

There are two possible threat points. In the case when abandoning the project completely is not a credible threat, then the Nash equilibrium (E^N) is the threat point: eschewing a private bargain does not mean giving up project implementation, but rather each party making decisions independently. In the case when one of the

---

[29] Project Cycle Management and Tacis Staffing (Evaluation Unit of DG 1A, 1997b, p.2).
[30] Project Cycle Management and Tacis Staffing (Evaluation Unit of DG 1A, 1997b, p.2).

parties can credibly threaten leaving the project, then $(0, 0)$ is the threat point. In either case, the bargaining equilibrium (E^B) will lie on the locus $\theta \phi_S R_L = k$, between the lines $\theta \phi(S) - k(|L - L^w|) = 0$ and $R(L) - S + S^w = R(0)$. None of the qualitative conclusions reached below is affected by which threat point pertains.

5. COMPARING EQUILIBRIA

The parties' rankings of outcomes under interest-group and embedded scenarios

To evaluate the properties of the equilibria, one must consider donor and recipient preferences. Assume that the recipient principal is motivated by political objectives, which establish the recipient principal's ordering over points in (S, L) space. These objectives reflect, for example, factors determining tenure in power. However, under (a possibly utopian) scenario, one might view the recipient principal's ordering as coincident with some notion of social welfare.

The donor's concerns are of two types. (For simplicity, this paper does not differentiate between the concerns of donor principal and donor agent. For insightful analysis of the consequences of this differentiation, see Seabright, Chapter 2.) Firstly, internal political pressures will force the donor to take into account the interests of the contractor. Secondly, whether for political or altruistic reasons, the donor cares about how recipients view outcomes. In some cases, the donor will use the recipient political leaders' judgments to assess how recipients view outcomes (recipient principal = political leaders). In other situations, the donor will have a view of what is best for the recipient populace (recipient principal = 'people').

These matters immediately raise the interpretation of $R(.)$. There are two distinct possibilities. In the 'interest group' case, there is a recipient-country principal–agent problem and the agent acts on behalf of some interest group, rather than in the interests of the principal. In the 'embedded' case, the productivity of the law depends on the fit between the character of the law and the characteristics of the recipient country. The interest group case is examined first, since that case has been most prominent in donor concerns.

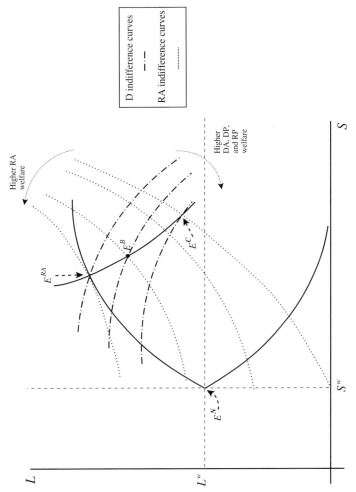

Figure 3.3. The ranking of equilibria in the interest-group case.

In the interest group case, $R(.)$ represents the political or even personal (bribes, political favours, etc.) payoff that the recipient agent receives for acting on behalf of some narrow interest. Perhaps $R(.)$ simply represents the specific bureaucratic interests of the recipient agent, for example in trying to minimise the administrative burden of implementing the new law. In any case, $R(.)$ does not represent the more general political interests of the recipient principal and certainly does not capture social benefits. To simplify analysis of the interest group case, assume that the Western law (L^w) is optimal for the recipient principal. One interpretation of this assumption is that the recipient political leaders want L^w. An alternative interpretation is that the donor has decided that its law is optimal for the recipient country, whatever the political leaders in the recipient country prefer, and that the donor has in mind some vague notion of the recipient 'people' as the true recipient principal and that it assumes that those people want the Western law.

In this interest-group case, the donor takes the recipient principal's preferred equilibrium as (S^w, L^w). If one assumes that deviations of L from L^W are particularly costly for the recipient principal (perhaps delaying EU accession), then the recipient principal's ordering of the equilibrium points is E^N, E^C, E^B, E^{RA} (most preferred listed first).[31] The ordering for the contractor is E^C, E^B, E^N, E^{RA} (with indifference between the last two). The recipient agent's ranking would be (E^{RA}, E^B, E^N, E^C). If the contractor does not loom too large in the donor principal's concerns, then the donor's ranking of equilibria will be the same as that of the recipient principal. This is the situation depicted in Figure 3.3. In this scenario, the optimal approach for the donor principal is splitting control over project decisions and preventing bargaining between the contractor and the recipient agent. If bargaining cannot be avoided, then the donor should place control in the hands of the contractor. *Ceteris paribus,*

---

[31] This ordering is equivalent to the assumption that the principal–agent problem in the recipient country is particularly acute. This would be the case, for example, if the deleterious effects of changes in the law were particularly important to the recipient principal, while the use of the recipient agent's captive resources, S, was not costly to the recipient principal. This scenario is particularly likely in a situation where the recipient agent is a powerful entrenched bureaucracy that is able to operate largely independently of the political system.

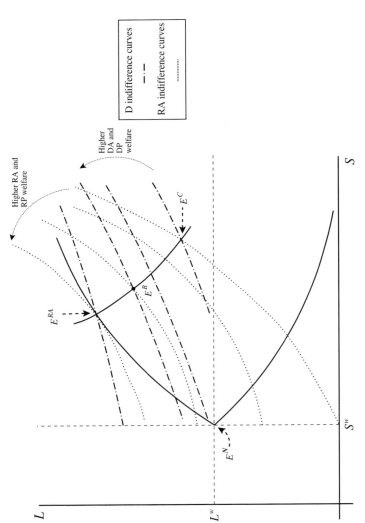

Figure 3.4. The ranking of equilibria in the embedded case.

enhancing the power of the contractor improves project outcomes from the perspective of the donor.

The interest group scenario is a natural one in the context of EU aid to a potential EU member that is acquiring the *Acquis Communitaire*. In aid projects in general, a common alternative scenario is when the Western law is not optimal for the recipient principal and the recipient principal benefits as L increases from L^w. This is the embedded case in which, to simplify the analysis, it is assumed that there is no principal–agent problem in the recipient country, implying that $R(.)$ reflects the benefits that the recipient principal derives from L (that is the benefits to the recipient principal, as well as to the recipient agent).

Now the political benefits of the recipient principal are an increasing function of $R(L) - S$. If the donor principal is concerned about the well-being of both the contractor and the recipient principal, donor welfare is a function of both $R(L) - S$ and $\theta\phi(S) - k$ ($|L - L^w|$). Thus, capturing the preferences of the recipient principal and the donor principal in the functions $u^{DP}(S, L)$ and $u^{RP}(S, L)$, the slopes of the indifference curves derived from these functions are related in the following manner: $(-u_L^{DP}/u_S^{DP}) > (-u_L^{RP}/u_S^{RP})$, in the pertinent region, that is where $(S, L) \geqq (S^w, L^w)$. From the point of view of the recipient principal, the order of ranking of the equilibrium points is E^{RA}, E^B, E^N, E^C (most preferred first). The ordering for the contractor is E^C, E^B, E^N, E^{RA} (with indifference between the last two). Therefore, virtually any ordering of these points is possible from the point-of-view of the donor, depending on how heavily the contractor's welfare is weighted.[32]

One plausible configuration appears in Figure 3.4, depicting a situation where the recipient's welfare counts strongly in the donor's preferences. Then, the ranking of the equilibrium points is the same for both donor and recipient principals and agents. In designing contractual arrangements, any move to give the recipient agent more control, *ceteris paribus*, would be endorsed by the donor principal. However, giving the recipient agent complete control entails two problems. Firstly, the contractor has the expertise to produce the law, so that control over the technical resources that produce

---

[32] But E^B will always be preferred to E^N.

L might naturally lie with the contractor. In that case, bargaining should be actively encouraged, with E^B being the best attainable solution. Secondly, and even more important, there has to be uncertainty concerning whether embeddedness is really the reason why the recipient agent wants to move L away from L^w. In fact, it might be the persuasive powers of interest groups that are the problem.

Some intermediate conclusions

The foregoing immediately suggests conclusions concerning the way in which the outcomes of foreign aid contracting are affected by the amount of information held by the parties, who is in control of project decisions, and the scope for post-contractual bargaining between contractor and recipient agent. Most critically, assessment of the different outcomes depends upon whether the recipient agent's interest in deviating from the Western-style law is because the project is an embedded one or because an interest-group has captured the recipient agent (the latter being a consequence of principal–agent problems in the recipient country).

In the interest-group case, the donor is concerned with reducing the possibility of post-contractual adjustments. If there is no possibility that bargaining would arise between the contractor and the recipient agent, then divided control of project decisions is optimal for the donor, leading to the implementation of the Nash equilibrium. Divided control is a rather natural arrangement. Contractor control of S would be viewed as intrusive in the recipient country, while the recipient agent does not have the knowledge to supervise the technical experts sent by the contractor to design L. If there is divided control, then in an interest group situation, the donor would want a consultant who is not familiar with the country, not for any technical reasons of project implementation, but rather because the contractor and the recipient agent are less likely to bargain to agreement if they are unfamiliar with each other. If efficiency in aid contracting occurs, one would expect to see situations where contractors unfamiliar with a country are given significant control over project decisions.

In the case of embeddedness, the donor has an interest in facilitating post-contractual adjustment, preferring the recipient agent to be in control of project decisions (unless the implementation of L^w is considered an absolute priority). Any move to give the recipient agent more control, *ceteris paribus*, results in an outcome that is viewed as better in the eyes of the donor. However, leaving the recipient agent in complete control of a project might be regarded as unusual, for the reasons offered in the previous paragraph: split control is the natural order. In that case, the donor would want to facilitate bargaining between the contractor and the recipient agent. Hence, in embedded project situations, the donor would want a consultant who is familiar with the country, not for any technical reasons of project design, but rather because a contractor and a recipient agent are more likely to be able to bargain to agreement when they are familiar with each other. In fact if the highest level of efficiency in aid contracting is to occur when embeddedness is the concern, one would expect to see situations where contractors familiar with a country are not given much control over decisions.

6. SOME ILLUSTRATIVE COMPARATIVE STATICS

There is already much implicit comparative statics in the above analysis. The model's results show the effects of variations in the type of institutional reform to be undertaken, different contractual conditions, and changes in the specifications of the roles of the recipient administration and the contractor. This section takes the comparative statics further by examining the effects of changes in the organisation of aid contracting. The examples of comparative statics were not simply conjured from the theory alone, but rather were suggested by the author's own knowledge of specific aid projects, gained both by observing contractors and recipients in the field and contractors and donors in Brussels and Washington.

Comparative statics 1: introducing evaluation

There is the possibility of observational feedback from the field to the donor. Let us view evaluation as providing such feedback.[33]

---

[33] Martens, Chapter 6, examines the role of evaluation in detail, stressing many of the problems in the process of evaluation. Here, since evaluation is not the focus, we ignore such problems.

Assume that the donor is particularly concerned about the effect of interest groups. (This case is particularly pertinent for projects funding the adoption of the *Acquis Communitaire* by a potential EU member.) Evaluators are charged with gathering information on whether L is close to L^w or not. This is information that is difficult to find. It is possible that the evaluators will not be able to obtain definitive evidence because the contractor can take actions to make the information less accessible. If found, however, such information will affect the contractor's reputation with the donor, affecting the award of future projects. (The incomplete contracts framework and the difficult observability of L suggest that information on L cannot be used to deny the contractor payment under the present contract, but rather that it will be used in the future as information on the contractor's reliability.)

This evaluation effect can be modeled in a simple manner. Firstly, when drafting an L that is different from L^w, the contractor will need to expend more energy in hiding differences and will therefore use more of its own resources. Secondly, the expected cost of the loss of reputation will depend on the probability that the evaluator correctly observes whether L is different from L^w or not. Plausibly, this probability is related to the difference between L and L^w. Therefore, the expected cost of the loss of reputation is a function of this difference. In both cases, the value of the parameter k increases. Assume as a result of both effects that k increases to k^+.[34]

One possible effect of the change in k is to rule out the possibility of any deviation from the E^N equilibrium. Remember that $\theta\phi_S(S^w)R_L(L^w) > k$ was a necessary condition for the possibility of moral hazard in contract implementation. A rise in k could lead to a reversal of the sign of this inequality, ruling out any post-contractual bargaining between the contractor and the recipient agent. This might be very productive in a situation where the donor is particularly concerned with interest groups thwarting the absorption of the *Acquis Communitaire*. Evaluation directly contributes to the improvement of contract outcomes from the point of view of the donor. Notice, however, that the effect of the evaluators

---

[34] Obviously, given that the change in k is partially due to a probabilistic effect, some non-linearities are being ignored.

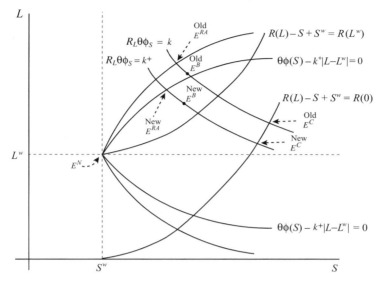

Figure 3.5. The effects of evaluation.

is implicit and cannot be easily observed: the very fact of their collecting information forestalls the occurrence of a bad equilibrium. Only the contractor can be really sure of the sequence of events.

Alternatively, $\theta\phi_S(S^w)R_L(L^w) > k^+$, in which case the equilibrium will depend on the particular specification of the contract. The effect of this change in k is depicted in Figure 3.5. (The changes in equilibria are denoted as shifts from 'old' to 'new'.) Both the locus of bargaining points and the contractor's participation constraint shift. Given the way in which the contractor's trade-off between L and S changes, these two effects will jointly have an ambiguous effect on S in the E^{RA} and E^B equilibria. S will decline in the E^C equilibrium. The effect on L is unambiguous: evaluation causes L to decline, which is exactly the effect sought when the chief focus of donor concern is the presence of recipient country interest groups trying to thwart the harmonisation of donor and recipient institutions and laws.

Comparative statics 2: introducing donor country NGOs

Contractors are either for-profit or not-for-profit entities. The distinction between these two is often inconsequential. The model above is cast in terms that are appropriate for the large majority of contractors, who have their eyes on the monetary bottom line.[35] But one type of not-for-profit organisation behaves very differently. This is a donor-country NGO interested in pushing a particular agenda. Examples might be a zealous environmental group or a group that favours one end of the political spectrum while working on a project for the implementation of democratic reforms. This sub-section assumes that the contractor is one such NGO.

Assume that the participation constraint of the NGO is the same as that of a not-for-profit organisation: $(\theta\phi(S) - k(|L - L^w|) \geqq 0$: there are no cross-project subsidies by the NGO. However, the NGO's specific objectives come into play when any rent on the project accrues. Those who work for the NGO will want the particular agenda of the NGO implemented, or as is quite often the case, those in the field will be particularly zealous proselytisers and will pursue the agenda even more strongly than the median NGO official. Assume that the NGO benefits, psychologically, from L deviating from L^w.

A simple way to model these preferences is through changes in k, which will now vary with (S, L). The parameter k has its usual value when the (S, L) combination is on the NGO's participation constraint, but k is smaller when the NGO earns a rent from the project because of the psychological reward that the NGO receives. The effect of the change in assumption is depicted in Figure 3.6. The only relationship changing position is the locus of points forming the bargaining set. Two of the equilibria do not change. NGOs and for-profit contractors produce the same outcomes when there is no bargaining during project implementation or when the recipient agent is in control of project implementation decisions.

---

[35] In the US, there are many not-for-profit contractors that are in the aid business that do not have a particular agenda. Such not-for-profit contractors can be analysed in the same way as for-profit contractors are.

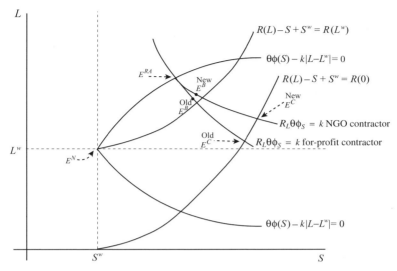

Figure 3.6. The effects of using NGOs as contractors.

Two equilibria do change, causing L and S to increase. When the NGO has enough bargaining power to earn rents, the willingness to take some of the rent in the form of increases in L directly results in more L and then indirectly, through the changed conditions of bargaining with the recipient agent, to even more L and more S.

It is tempting to assume that the above situation depicts one where the well-being of participants has improved, given the aura that surrounds NGOs, especially in the present aid environment. But NGOs have a specific agenda: they are an interest group. They might simply strengthen the effects of recipient country interest groups, whose goals do not coincide with those of recipient principal or donor principal. For example, in environmental legislation, standards and regulations might be legislated that are too stringent to be justified on economic grounds. This is not an unfamiliar phenomenon to those who have witnessed Cadillac-environmentalists (or perhaps, now, Lexus-environmentalists) who descend on the pristine territory of a poor nation. Similarly, the author has witnessed western NGOs distorting the results of elections, when given a mandate simply to teach the techniques of democracy.

Comparative statics 3: contractor capture of the donor agent

Outside the framework of a particular project, contractors can improve the donor agent's situation in a number of ways: offering post-retirement employment, doing some of the work of the donor agent, helping to enhance the reputation of the donor agent in the eyes of the donor principal, etc. Thus, when the principal–agent problem in the donor country is particularly acute, the contractor might 'capture' the donor agent: the donor agent becomes the agent of the contractor rather than of the donor principal.

This case is particularly easy to analyse because its effects are simply the opposite of those in the first comparative statics case. To see this point, consider the fact that the contractor has two strategies. The contractor can expend its resources on hiding differences between L and L^w and risk the possible loss of reputation when its malfeasance is discovered by the donor agent. Or, the contractor can expend its resources on fostering a compliant donor agent, in the manner suggested in the previous paragraph. In this latter case, there will be two effects on k. The parameter k will decrease because the contractor will need to do less to hide the fact that it has designed an L that is far from L^w. However, k will increase because the costs of deviating from L^w now include a cost of maintaining a compliant donor agent (which are related to $|L - L^w|$ since it is more difficult for the donor agent to hide the contractor's problems from superiors as the contractor's malfeasance increases.) If the second effect is less than the first, then there is a decline in k and the contractor chooses to nurture a compliant donor agent. With the donor agent now exerting less vigilant oversight over the contractor's performance, the change is from the 'new' to the 'old' points in Figure 3.5. In particular, L will increase: the lack of vigilance on the part of the donor agent strengthens the effects of the interest groups in the recipient country, a situation that is costly when the donor has a strong desire to implement L^w. The progress of Western-funded privatisation programs in transition countries could be fruitfully studied with this comparative statics exercise.

*Comparative statics 4: the recipient agent influences the
donor agent's views of the contractor*

Drafting legislation is quite often a technical exercise. Getting the
legislation passed involves the art of politics. The contractor spe-
cialises in the former, the recipient agent in the latter. However,
the contract between donor and contractor often specifies that the
contractor should produce legislation that can be passed. If there
is a problem, then the contractor might forfeit part of the monies
due on the contract, or lose reputation and therefore future contracts. Therefore, in situations where the donor agent cannot collect
enough information on why legislation stalls, the recipient agent
might be able to threaten to sully the contractor's reputation by
delaying the passage of legislation or even blocking it.

This scenario raises many complicated issues of bargaining between the contractor and the recipient agent, because it extends the
domain of bargaining from the pre-implementation stage, which
is the one that has been considered so far, to the time period when
the project is being implemented, after the contractor and the recipient agent have already committed some resources. Therefore,
a full investigation of this phenomenon would involve modelling
a sequential bargaining process, a completely different modelling
structure than the one presently used. But by providing a suggestive
analysis using the present model, it is possible to offer an intuitive
understanding of what happens when the recipient agent influences
the donor agent's view of the contractor.

Effectively, if the recipient can sully the contractor's reputation, it
has more to offer to the contractor when project decisions are being
made. This can be modelled as an increase in θ. The recipient agent
has a particularly productive way of using its resources on behalf of
the contractor: it can lobby the donor agent for the benefit of the
contractor. The effects of this are simple to see because raising θ has
the same effect on relationships as lowering k. Therefore, when the
donor agent listens to the recipient agent's views on the contractor
this is equivalent to the move from the 'new' to the 'old' equilibria
in Figure 3.5. L will increase in all equilibria (except E^N).

In comparing this case and the previous one, an apparent paradox arises. When the contractor gains by capturing the donor agent,

the equilibrium value of L changes in the same direction as when the contractor loses because the recipient agent can affect the contractor's reputation. The paradox is resolved by noting that these changes have one factor in common: they increase the scope for bargaining between the recipient agent and the contractor by reducing the cost of what the contractor can give to the recipient agent or what the recipient agent can give to the contractor. Of course, which cost is reduced affects the distribution of rents from the project, but the effect on what the donor most cares about, L, is the same.

One real-world application of this last comparative statics exercise arose in transition countries. Those who worked in such countries were often surprised that aid projects were implemented less well when the young westernised reformers were in control than when the old-line communists were in charge. This seemed paradoxical because the reformers' objectives were certainly more in line with those of the donors and the reformers had better knowledge of market economies. However, the reformers also had the power to influence the opinions of the donor agents, possibly with the results predicted in the previous paragraphs.

7. SEPARATING EMBEDDED AND INTEREST GROUP PROJECTS

To this point, the only differences between the embedded and interest group cases have been in interpreting how the participants evaluate different outcomes, not in predicting which case will actually occur. The modelling of the behaviours of the recipient agent and the contractor and the factors that affect them have been exactly the same in the two cases. Therefore, predictions about the equilibria will be the same. However, there is one aspect of the model where a natural difference between the two cases arises, in the productivity of local resources in producing institutional reform. Aid-project procedures, both contract design and evaluation, can take advantage of this difference.

In the interest group case, the most productive outcome is to have *de jure* law equal to *de facto* law equal to the prevailing Western law. In this scenario, where embeddedness is assumed not to be an important factor, the local landscape is relatively easy to map and to traverse. This is a matter of comparative, not absolute, costs: the paper simply assumes that embeddedness is a situation where the costs of dealing with local idiosyncracies are very high, not that these costs are absent in the interest group case. Nevertheless, one can use the simplifying assumption that the resources, S, are simply a payoff to persuade the contractor to create the divergence between *de jure* and *de facto* law. Therefore, S is used for a purpose that has low productivity for recipient country citizens, to provide benefits to the contractor.

In the embedded case, the resources provided by the recipient agent will be much more productive. Local personnel are needed to interpret local institutions, formal and informal. The character of the social system might be much less obvious to an outsider than to an insider. Moreover, where complementarity between institutional reform and existing institutions is important, local labour is very productive, in securing appropriate agreements with recipient organisations not directly involved in the project and in making sure that the design fits the local landscape. These factors are not absent in the interest group case, but they are assumed to be much more important in the embeddedness scenario.

Thus, in the embedded case, S is a payoff to the contractor, as in the interest group case, but more importantly it is also a provision of essential inputs for the contractor's project work. Local resources, S, are relatively more productive in the embedded case than in the interest group case. The parameter θ has been included in the model in order to capture this difference. In the embedded case, $\theta = \theta_e$ and in the interest group case $\theta = \theta_i$, with $\theta_e > \theta_i$.[36]

The model then has some of the elements of the standard adverse selection model.[37] The donor wants to offer aid projects and two types of recipient agents want to receive them. The aid project in its standard form is beneficial for both types. Thus, the standard aid contract will lead to a pooling equilibrium. But the donor might prefer an outcome that used a set of contracts that will separate the two types of the recipient agent. Optimal separating contracts would implement E^N in the interest group case and E^{RA} in the

---

[36] Rudner's (1991, p.16) description of Canada's 1988 revamping of its development process suggests an attempt to differentiate between embedded and interest group projects.

[37] See Salanié (1997, Chapters 2 and 3) for an exposition in the context of contract theory.

embedded case. If optimality is not attainable, then other forms of separation might improve on the pooling equilibrium from the point of view of the donor. Perhaps, when the concern is particularly with interest groups thwarting the absorption of the *Acquis Communitaire*, aid procedures might aim at minimising the dangers posed by interest groups. This case is examined in the ensuing example.

Example 1: minimising the effects of interest groups

For the purposes of the remainder of this section, assume that all projects are identical except for the parameter θ, which has two different values θ_e and θ_i. Let S_j^k be the value of S when $\theta = \theta_j$ $(j = i, e)$ and when equilibrium k occurs $(k = RA, C, N, \text{or } B)$. L_j^k is similarly defined. It is easy to show that: $\theta_e \phi(S_e^k) - k|L_e^k - L^w| > \theta_i \phi(S_i^k) - k|L_i^k - L^w|$ for $k = C$. That is, when the recipient agent has no bargaining power and the contractor is able to stipulate project decisions, the contractor is better off under an embedded arrangement than under an interest group situation.

Thus, project arrangements could stipulate that the contractor should be in control of project decisions and that the donor payment to the contractor should equal $K - G$, where $G > 0$. There is a value of G at which no interest group projects will be implemented. But if G is set too low and interest group projects are funded, then they will be implemented at E^C, the best outcome for the donor in the interest group case (apart from the Nash equilibrium, which cannot be obtained with any certainty unless bargaining can be ruled out).

Example 2: aiming for an optimum allocation of limited aid funds

The arrangements suggested in the previous example eliminate the possibility of poor outcomes from the point of view of the donor when decisions (on G) are made incorrectly. An alternative strategy would be to aim to obtain the donor's preferred outcome when decisions are made correctly, risking very poor outcomes if miscalculations are made in setting project parameters.

The donor agent could stipulate that the recipient agent should be in control of all project decisions. In return, the recipient agent should pay a fee to the donor equal to F, where $F > 0$.

As $R(L_e^k) - S_e^k > R(L_i^k) - S_i^k$ for $k = RA$, we know that there is a value of F at which no interest group projects will be implemented, because if F is set correctly, the recipient agent would be better off at $(0, 0)$ than at (S_i^{RA}, L_i^{RA}). This result explains the rather puzzling phenomenon that recipients are often asked to co-finance development projects. But it also shows that this fee should be linked to the control of the project by recipient agents.

8. CASE STUDIES

The reader who has observed or participated in aid projects will surely recognise predictions of the model that resonate with experience. Nevertheless, for those with less practical experience, it might be useful to apply the model to some simple case studies, to show how closely the model mirrors reality. (Indeed, the author's own personal experiences led to the model.) The subsections below contain three examples of real-world applications. As any such application will usually characterise the malfeasance or turpitude of some actor, the examples are presented in a manner that disguises who the actors and countries are. The purpose here is not to indict, but to amplify. The fictitious country names are the same in all subsections, but in fact both donor and recipient countries vary across examples.

Case study 1: the consequences of using the contractor to blunt the influence of interest groups

During the early transition process, Ruritania was rife with interest groups. Officials in Munificentia, the donor country, were terribly worried about the deleterious effects of such groups on reform. These officials thought that embeddedness was of no importance. Spurred by perceived political urgency, Munificentia gave a large amount of aid to Ruritania through a prestigious contractor stipulating that the contractor control project decisions. The contractor had a very credible image in both Munificentia and Ruritania and was able to convert this control into significant influence over policy in Ruritania.

This programme has now come under great criticism. Two criticisms in particular surface. Firstly, the reforms implemented under this aid project have not produced obvious gains, critics commenting not on any incompetence on the part of the contractor, but rather focusing on the fact that the contractor does not seem to have made accurate predictions concerning how their programmes would work in the Ruritanian environment. Within Ruritania, there is constant criticism that the reforms did not fit the Ruritanian context. Secondly, there have been allegations that the contractor profited too much from this programme and was able to use project resources for activities that benefited the contractor rather than Ruritania. Critics claim that each of these two problems emanates from the fact that the contractor was given too much control over the programme.

Our model allows us to see that Munificentia's original decision to give control to the contractor was completely defensible under the assumption that interest groups were a real danger in Ruritania. The Ruritanian critics of project outcomes simply have a different opinion on the relative importance of the embeddedness and interest group assumptions. Given the vesting of control in the contractor, it was inevitable that L would be chosen closer to L^w than considered appropriate by those who think that embeddedness was important (compare E^C to E^{RA}). Hence, the criticisms that the projects did not fit the context in which they were applied. Moreover, given the contractor's control, the contractor would surely earn rents by constructing agreements with representatives of Ruritanian interest groups or specific political or bureaucratic interests. The contractor might have been unwise to use these rents indiscreetly, but their existence was a direct consequence of contractual arrangements, which officials in Munificentia would claim were absolutely necessary given the circumstances in Ruritania. The criticisms of this programme should not focus on project implementation arrangements but judgments on the importance of interest groups and embeddedness in Ruritania.

Case study 2: the importance of project governance when
there is embeddedness

The contractor was given control of a programme of economics and legal education in Ruritania. In this case, L^w could be interpreted as a 'Western' education and deviations from L^w could be interpreted as recasting that education to make its lessons more pertinent for the Ruritanian context. In return for recasting the program in such a way, the contractor received facilitative help (that is, S in terms of the model) from officials in Ruritania. The contractor earned a surplus from this program, but because the contractor was a non-profit one this surplus was converted into two non-monetary benefits for the contractor. Firstly, the contractor increased project quality more than was contractually needed (see Comparative statics 2 p.98). This increase in quality enhanced the contractor's reputation, leading to further contracts from the donor. Secondly, some of the educators were able to use project resources to conduct research to increase their own human capital. By using an embedded situation to its advantage when it was in control of decisions, the contractor was able both to earn a surplus and to gain a reputation for implementing a successful project.

On a follow-on project, the donor agent from Munificentia decided that a 'real partnership' was needed between the recipient agent and the contractor. The donor agent made this decision using an analysis that could be phrased in terms of embeddedness. Control over project decisions was now split between the recipient agent and the contractor. However, the mechanisms of project governance were set up in a manner that did not allow productive bargaining between the recipient agent and the contractor. The project was implemented in a perfunctory manner with embeddedness hardly taken into account in creating L (the education). The equilibrium of this second project was E^N in contrast to the E^C equilibrium of the first project: the welfare of all parties had declined. The donor agent, by not taking into account bargaining during implementation, produced changes in the organization of the second project that led to changes in outputs that were the opposite of those desired.

*Case study 3: Haste makes waste when it affects
the control of projects*

The contractor from Munificentia came to Ruritania in a hurry. Munificentia wanted to be seen as acting quickly in this poor country, which was becoming ever more desperate for aid.

(Munificentians had inherited some overdue commitments from a previous political era.) The contractor had to act quickly and had little knowledge of the local environment. This gave the recipient agent control of project decisions. The recipient agent gave the contractor quick implementation of the project. (An S similar to that in Comparative statics 3 p. 100.) In return, L was far away from L^w in a situation in which embeddedness had no role. Now, while the actors in this project have gone on to other activities, the costs are still with Munificentia. The interest groups saddled state enterprises with unwanted loans under this project and the loans were channeled through the banking system. Now, a privatised enterprise sector is deeply indebted, a banking sector has non-performing assets, and there is standstill in credit markets. When a contractor enters a new environment with a charge to do things quickly, project control will inevitably be in the hands of the recipient agent because of informational advantages. Sometimes, as in this example, the aid project will inflict tremendous costs on the 'beneficiary' nation.

9. CONCLUSIONS: LESSONS LEARNED

The purpose of the present chapter has been to use standard economic tools to model the process of aid-project implementation, focusing on the role of the independent contractor. Such a model must embody a multiplicity of factors – the role of the donor agent, the incomplete contract given to the contractor, variations in the locus of project control, a characterisation of the preferences of the participants over project outputs, a role for interest groups and for embeddedness, the possibility of moral hazard in project implementation, and a specification of the bargaining process between recipient agent and contractor. In addition, in order to be most useful, the model should admit the possibility of comparative-statics exercises that reflect changes in the environment that surround project implementation. Thus, the model should allow incorporation of evaluation and monitoring, contractor capture of the donor agent, NGOs as contractors, etc. The model presented in this paper does all of this while maintaining a tractability that facilitates the derivation of results that reflect upon the reality of aid processes, as the case studies in the previous section attest.

The most important conclusion of this paper is the one implicit in the previous paragraph – the application of standard economic tools in analysing aid processes can be productive and can offer insights that improve the effectiveness of foreign-aid giving. The model's results could be used to reflect on aid project design, the structure of aid contracts, and the role of evaluation and monitoring.

Although the modelling exercise is the most important output of this paper – showing how some applied theory can elucidate important phenomena – some of the particular conclusions reached above are worthy of emphasis. In particular:

- Contractual details do matter – the effectiveness of project implementation is greatly influenced by decisions on who controls which aspects of a project.
- Information relevant to judging whether a project is effective is revealed by the nature of the resources contributed to the project by the recipient agent. Evaluation can use this information.
- The work of evaluators can improve project outcomes by changing the incentives of the actors.
- Whether the contractor is an NGO or profit-seeking consultant can change the effectiveness of project implementation.
- The history of the previous relationship between the contractor and the recipient matters, because it will affect the possibility that a bargaining outcome is reached.
- There is great paradox in the optimal configuration of the control of aid projects. If efficiency is the goal, one would expect to see contractors who are unfamiliar with a country given control of projects and contractors who are familiar with a country given less control. The paradox is resolved by noting that contractor control is most useful in those situations where bargaining should be discouraged and bargaining should be encouraged when contractor control is least useful.[38]
- The optimal configuration of the project implementation arrangements, from the point of view of the donor, depends critically on whether embeddedness or interest group influence is particularly important in the project being implemented.

---

[38] Of course, this conclusion depends upon the assumption maintained in the body of the paper, that contractors do not vary in their ability to deliver the donor's objectives.

- The efficiency of the set of projects selected for implementation can be greatly affected by the fees paid to contractors and the contributions expected of recipient agencies.

REFERENCES

Binmore, Ken (1992) *Fun and Games: a Text on Game Theory.* Lexington, MA: D.C. Heath.

Claque, Christopher C. (ed.) (1997) *Institutions and Economic Development: Growth and Governance in Less-Developed and Post-Socialist Countries.* Baltimore: Johns Hopkins University Press.

Evaluation Unit of the Directorate General for External Relations (DG 1A) of the European Commission (1997a) *Phare: an Interim Evaluation.* Brussels: European Commission.

Evaluation Unit of the Directorate General for External Relations (DG 1A) of the European Commission (1997b) *Tacis Interim Evaluation Synthesis Report.* Brussels: European Commission.

Granovetter, Mark S. (1985) Economic action and social structure: the problem of embeddedness. *American Journal of Sociology*, 91, 481–510.

Grossman, Sanford and Hart, Oliver (1986) The costs and benefits of ownership: a theory of vertical and lateral integration. *Journal of Political Economy*, XCIV, 691–719.

Hart, Oliver and Moore, John (1990) Property rights and the nature of the firm. *Journal of Political Economy*, XCVIII, 1119–58.

Hart, Oliver *et al.* (1997) The proper scope of government: theory and an application to prisons. *Quarterly Journal of Economics*, 112(4), 1127–61.

Kanbur, Ravi, and Sandler, Todd (1999) *The Future of Development Assistance: Common Pools and International Public Goods.* Washington DC: Policy Essay No. 25. Overseas Development Council.

Klugt, Arianne Beetsma-van der, Phedon Nicolaides, Christophe Soulard and Alexander Türk (1997) An Assessment of the Approximation Process in Poland: the Importance of Coordination and Enforcement. Paper prepared for the European Commission, Maastricht, March 1997.

Laffont, Jean-Jacques and Tirole, Jean (1993) *A Theory of Incentives in Procurement and Regulation.* Cambridge, MA: MIT Press.

Martens, Bertin (1998) *Developing a Methodology for the Evaluation of Institution Building and Reform Projects.* Directorate General 1A, Brussels: European Commission.

North, Douglass C. (1990) *Institutions, Institutional Change, and Economic Performance.* Cambridge: Cambridge University Press.

Pietrobelli, Carlo and Scarpa, Carlo (1992). Inducing efficiency in the use of foreign aid: the case of incentive mechanisms. *Journal of Development Studies*, 29(1), 72–92.

Putzel, James (1998) The business of aid: transparency and accountability in European Union development assistance. *Journal of Development Studies*, 34(3), 71–96.

Rudner, Martin (1991) Canada's official development assistance strategy: process, goals, priorities. *Canadian Journal of Development Studies*, 12(1), 9–37.

Salanié, Bernard (1997) *The Economics of Contracts: a Primer*. Cambridge, MA: MIT Press.

Schmidt, Klaus M. (1996) The costs and benefits of privatization: an incomplete contracts approach. *Journal of Law, Economics, Organization*, (12)1, 1–24.

Shapiro, Carl and Willig, Robert D. (1990) Economic rationales for the scope of privatization. In: Suleiman, Ezra and Waterbury, John (eds.) *The Political Economy of Private Sector Reform and Privatization*, pp. 55–87, Boulder, CO: Westerview.

Shleifer, Andrei, and Vishny, Robert W. (1994) Politicians and firms. *Quarterly Journal of Economics*, 109(4), 995–1026.

Tirole, Jean (1994) The internal organization of government. *Oxford Economic Papers*, 46, 1–29.

White, Howard and Morrissey, Oliver O. (1997) Conditionality when donor and recipient preferences vary. *Journal of International Development*, 9(4), 497–505.

4

Embedding externally induced institutional reforms

Uwe Mummert

1. INTRODUCTION

The previous chapter examined the likelihood of formal acceptance of institutional reforms, proposed by a foreign donor agency,
by a recipient country government. It was shown that this depends on the contractual arrangements between donors, private
contractors and recipient organisations. Asymmetric information
flows in the implementation process could easily derail the proposed reforms from their target, unless the reform movement and
the recipient country counterpart institutions are well embedded
in the local political environment. In this chapter we move one
step further in the delivery process of donor-financed institutional
reform programmes and examine what happens inside the recipient country, once a reform proposed by an external donor agency
has been formally – *de jure* – accepted by the recipient country
government. It offers an abstraction of the agency problems that
may occur upstream of *de jure* acceptance and concentrates on the
downstream *de facto* behaviour of citizens. It focuses on endogenous
processes that determine the effectiveness of institutional reforms,
once they have been formally adopted by governments. Formal or
de jure reform in itself is a necessary but not a sufficient condition
for effective application of reforms.

   In order to facilitate impersonal exchange in modern market economies, an effective framework of formal institutions is
required.[1] Wide-ranging institutional reforms are therefore an

The author gratefully acknowledges support for this study from the European Commission's
Tacis programme.
[1] We define institutions as rules that are endowed with an enforcement mechanism. Their
   enforcement mechanism can be used as a distinction criterion (Buchanan 1975: 118,

integral part of many reform programmes in developing and transition countries. 'Normal' institutional reform processes are generated endogenously in countries, through a variety of social, economic and political forces. Foreign donor-induced reforms however, have an exogenous source and are not necessarily rooted in domestic forces. The importance of this subject reaches far beyond the vast transfer of European Union (EU) legislation to the EU's candidate member states in Central and Eastern Europe. It includes all cases where domestic governments have agreed to carry out institutional reforms in order to fulfill their international obligations, such as those under structural adjustment programmes supported by the International Monetary Fund (IMF) and the World Bank, or reforms related to membership of the World Trade Organisation (WTO) or other international trade agreements.

Recent research into the conditions for successful donor-induced reform has provided evidence that instrumental variables controlled by donor agencies have little impact on the success or failure of reforms. Dollar and Svensson (1998) demonstrate that donors can at best encourage reforms and offer models of 'foreign' institutions as guidance. Successful reform depends primarily on micro-level processes inside the recipient countries and their organisations, after a government has formally agreed to implement a particular institutional reform. This chapter explores these *de facto* micro-level processes, after a reform is adopted *de jure* by the recipient country or organization. Thus, we focus on the 'embeddedness' of reforms in the wider socio-economic environment. Granovetter (1985) argued that most economic and social transactions do not take place between anonymous agents but between agents who are part of social networks. Similarly, government agencies and their agents are embedded in a concrete set of social ties, informal institutions and social networks, that binds them to society and influences the way in which they implement the reforms. Thomas and Grindle (1990) argue that the outcome of formal institutional reform programmes is not so much determined by reactions in the public and political realm but largely by the reactions of

Ostrom, 1986, Ellickson, 1991, Knight, 1992). Formal institutions like constitutions, laws or regulations rest on the state's enforcement power. Informal institutions by contrast are enforced by private actors. Examples include social norms or customs.

agencies and officials in the bureaucratic arena (see also Naím, 1995).

This chapter concentrates on the process of implementing institutional reforms and the role of public agencies therein. We assume that the recipient government formally adopts the institutional reforms proposed by the foreign donor and that no moral hazard occurs in this respect. The respective laws or regulations have been passed by the legislature and our analysis is concentrated on the reasons why reforms may nevertheless fail, due to divergent interests by the public agencies that implement them and by private actors that are to follow the rules.

In Section 2, a principal–agent model is presented that traces the characteristics of the 'implementation game' of *de jure* reforms. Three players are involved: a formal government authority that declares the law and delegates implementation responsibilities to a public administration agent who supervises the behaviour of citizens or constituent agents who should behave in accordance with the law.

Although the notion of conflict between formal institutions and indigenous social norms, as an important factor in the failure of institutional reforms, seems to be almost common sense within the institutional-theoretical literature (North, 1981, p.53; North, 1990, p.45; Cooter, 1997, p.192; Pejovich, 1997, p.246; Aoki, 1998, p.5), a detailed analysis of possible conflict situations and their likely outcomes is still lacking. Thus, Sections 3 and 4 take a more substantive look at possible conflicts between formal and informal institutions. We identify two main areas of conflict. Firstly, a direct conflict between formal and informal institutions may emerge because of contradicting contents of the respective institutions leading to rule-violating behaviour. In section 3 it is argued that the degree of prescriptiveness of institutions, their legitimacy and the structure of social networks decide over the quality of the relationship between formal and informal institutions. Even in the absence of a direct conflict between formal and informal institutions, the latter may still hinder the application of *de jure* granted entitlements. Secondly, in Section 4, we move to indirect conflict situations between formal and informal institutions. In this case we will not so much observe rule-violating behaviour but rather a reluctance to use the positive freedoms granted by formal market institutions. This affects wealth accumulation and may result in a lesser acceptance of institutional reforms, because their main benefits are not realised for the majority of private actors.

Obviously, the more stable the conflicting informal institutions, the more endangered the formal institutional reforms. Thus, assessment of the problems of embedding institutional reforms requires not only a search for conflicting social norms, but also a measurement of the degree of persistency they might present in the course of institutional reforms. This task will be tackled in Section 5. Finally, the main findings of this chapter as well as some policy implications are presented in Section 6.

2. THE IMPLEMENTATION GAME[2]

If a government could fully observe the behaviour of the agencies to whom it delegates implementation responsibilities, there would be no problem in turning *de jure* into *de facto* rules. However, this is a rather unrealistic assumption. Ample empirical evidence points to the power of information asymmetries with respect to the relationship between governments and their agencies (Downs, 1967/1994, Wilson, 1989). Public agencies can change policies in subtle ways and thus alter the implementation modalities of reforms.

Effective implementation of laws and regulations requires a range of inputs from various agents. A public administration has to put the legislation in concrete terms and to establish corresponding procedural rules. If new domains of regulation are concerned, public agencies may have to be built up from scratch. Furthermore, jurisdictional agencies (the police, prosecuting attorneys, courts) have to prosecute and sanction violations of the law and finally the constituents have to comply with the new law. Opportunism or open violation of agency contracts may impede effectiveness.

Public agents may have various motives not to behave in accordance with their instructions. Firstly, effort is always costly. Agents have to learn the new laws and application procedures. Bureaucratic routines may turn obsolete or resources may be cut

---

[2] With apologies to Eugene Bardach. We could not resist copying the title of his (1977) illustrative analysis of what happens after a bill becomes a law.

down. Current wages or future prospects may be reduced and specific investments may be devalued. Reforms may diverge from the agency's own political agenda. Secondly, besides these direct effects on public agents' utility, additional indirect effects may exist because public agents do not implement reforms in isolation. They are constantly interacting with other constituents, i.e. family, friends, neighbours, customers, anonymous citizens, etc. The outcome of that bargaining game may result in collusive behaviour that impedes the effectiveness of reforms. Constituents may also experience costs as a result of the reforms. Income losses or devaluation of specific investments constitute motives for individual actors to object to reforms. As a result, they may be inclined to exert pressure on public agents' utility in order to impede the implementation of the law.

Economic interests

In order to clarify the stakes of the parties involved, we will draw on a model developed by Mookherjee and Png (1995).[3] The agency approach to organisation theory rests on the assumption that a principal can induce co-operative behaviour among his agents, despite imperfect information about their behaviour, provided he introduces the right incentives in the contract that links him to his agents. We will examine to what extent collective action by the public agents and/or the supervised citizens to protect their rents can overturn the incentives offered by the government principal (Laffont and Rochet, 1997, p.485).

We identify two representative players in the game: a citizen or constituent who should comply with the new formal institution and a public agent who has to supervise compliance. The new law may either prescribe or prohibit an action, which may involve an individual welfare loss. Hence, the constituent may decide not to behave accordingly and take some action a that differs from the provisions in the law. Thus, a denotes a violation. It avoids a cost or constitutes a private gain for the constituent, denoted as $\pi(a)$. It is assumed that $\pi(0) = 0$, $\pi(a)$ is strictly increasing, strictly concave, and differentiable.

---

[3] For other models focusing on collusive behaviour between agents, see Tirole, 1986, Tirole, 1992, Laffont and Tirole, 1993, Laffont and Rochet, 1997.

According to law, violation is sanctioned by a penalty P^a. The public agent has discretion regarding the extent to which he implements the new institution. He may sanction the observed violation a only partially. Thus, the penalty is based on a smaller violation ($\tilde{a}$) than the actually performed violation (a). It is further assumed that the public agent receives a reward of r dollars which depends on his enforcement and thus on the amount of sanction imposed on the constituent ($P^a\tilde{a}$). It is also assumed that the public agent will never sanction an action of the constituent that has actually not taken place. Thus $\tilde{a} \leq a$.

If the constituent does not comply with the new rule, he may have an interest in urging the public agent to enforce only a lower level of non-compliance ($\tilde{a}$). By this, the constituent can reduce his penalty from $P^a a$ to $P^a\tilde{a}$. However, this will reduce the income that the public agent receives from the state as $rP^a\tilde{a} < rP^a a$.

If the public agent chooses to sanction only $P^a\tilde{a}$ in stead of $P^a a$ it may happen that the information about the bribe and the true extent of violation a of the constituent leaks to other state authorities with an exogenous probability ρ. If the corruption is discovered, the constituent not only has to pay the amount of penalty evaded, $P^a(a - \tilde{a})$, but suffers an additional penalty for giving a bribe at a rate P^b_g making a total of $(1 + P^b_g)P^a(a - \tilde{a})$. The public agent will be penalised for inadequate implementation and for taking a bribe $P^b_t(a - \tilde{a})$. Thus, the constituent expects to gain from a bribe $P^a(a - \tilde{a})[1 - \rho(1 + P^b_g)]$. The bribe creates for the public agent the utility b and for the constituent the cost b.

If the public agent fully enforces the new rule, he will receive an official income $rP^a a$ from the government. If, however, he takes a bribe and reduces enforcement, his official income will decrease to $rP^a\tilde{a}$. Furthermore, with probability ρ he will be penalised $P^b_t(a - \tilde{a})$. Therefore, bargaining between the constituent and the public agent will take place if and only if both can benefit from it, that is, the following inequality has to be fulfilled.

$$(a - \tilde{a})\left(rP^a + \rho P^b_t\right) < \left\{P^a(a - \tilde{a})\left[1 - \rho\left(1 + P^b_g\right)\right]\right\} \quad (4.1)$$

The left side of the inequality denotes the loss of income the public agent suffers from not fully implementing the rule plus the potential penalty for being caught for inadequate enforcement.

The right side of the inequality denotes the net gain of the constituent in case of prevented full implementation. It is the gain for not being fully penalised for performing activity a plus the potential penalty for being caught giving bribes to the public agent.

The actual outcome of the bargaining process – the bribe – depends on the relative power of the parties involved. However, it is common to derive the outcome of a bargaining process using the Nash bargaining solution. Thus, assuming equal bargaining power, the bribe is a function of the extent of violation a, the potential penalties both actors face and the probabilities of being discovered while colluding:

$$b = 1/2 \left\{ \left[1 - \rho \left(1 + P_g^b \right) + r \right] P^a + \rho P_t^b \right\} a \qquad (4.2)$$

Hence, an individual constituent may pay the public agent in order to avoid effective institutional reform. However, very likely a single individual will not be sufficient to prevent *de facto* institutional reform since implementation usually requires a multitude of different public agents. Therefore, the actor would have to bribe many public agents, which will become quite expensive. The chances of avoiding implementation are much higher if the constituents manage to achieve some collective action and exert massive influence on public agents to cheat on implementation. Organised individuals can offer higher monetary side transfers than a single actor. Furthermore, they may be able to affect not only a single public agent but several. Thus, it is of crucial importance for *de facto* institutional change whether the constituents manage to accomplish collective action. Let n denote the number of constituents who are willing to engage in collective action in order to exert a massive influence on the public agent. It is quite obvious that the higher n, the lower is the cost the individual actor has to bear for side payments $(1/nb)$. This turns inequality (4.1) into:

$$(a - \tilde{a}) \left(rP^a + \rho P_t^b \right) < n \left\{ P^a \left(a - \tilde{a} \right) \left[1 - \rho \left(1 + P_g^b \right) \right] \right\} \qquad (4.3)$$

Thus, if there is widespread opposition among the constituents to effective reform and if they manage to organise themselves it is much more likely that the necessary precondition for collusion between the public agent and the constituent will be fulfilled. This is particularly true if an institutional reform negatively affects constituents who are already organised. In this case the interest groups are likely to capture the public agencies and boycott institutional reform.

So far, we have concentrated on more or less anonymous market corruption. However, much more persistent and pervasive is parochial corruption which is the result of the embeddedness of public agents in social networks. Therefore, we have to analyse to what extent the informal social networks in which public agents are involved may present an obstacle for the implementation.

Informal institutions

Social networks are endowed with a set of informal institutions, rules that are not sanctioned by government but rather through social interaction. Researchers have become increasingly aware of their power and ability to reduce the efficacy of formal institutions (North, 1981, p.53; North, 1990, p.45; Cooter, 1997, p.192; Pejovich, 1997, p.246; Aoki, 1998, p.5; Voigt and Kiwit, 1998, p.91). If social sanctions generated by informal institutions result in the rejection of new formal institutions, this poses an even more serious obstacle to reform than outright bribery.

As these social networks existed prior to the reforms, there is no collective action hurdle and no need to urge public agents to relax implementation standards for reforms. Furthermore, these shared informal institutions facilitate bargaining regarding (partial) noncompliance (Elster, 1989). Thus, the reward for public agents for enforcing the formal law will be reduced by costs (c) that are imposed through social sanctions: $r' = r - c$. This reduces the left side of inequality (4.1) and makes the necessary conditions for collusive behaviour more likely:

$$(a - \tilde{a}) \left(r' P^a + \rho P_t^b \right) < \left\{ P^a \left(a - \tilde{a} \right) \left[1 - \rho \left(1 + P_g^b \right) \right] \right\} \quad (4.4)$$

Additionally, through equation (4.2) the reduced reward r' will result in lower bribes. Hence, the price of not complying with the law decreases. If informal sanctions are sufficiently strong they may totally replace bribing. This would change the structure of the game compared to bribing. Many informal sanctions such as shunning are not subject to penalties by the state, i.e. $P_t^b = 0$. Moreover, it is quite likely that the agent adheres to social norms and does not require much social pressure.

So far, we have analysed the different causes of agency problems that may be responsible for an imperfect implementation of laws or regulations that are transplanted by institutional reform programmes. The analysis shows that conflict between formal and informal institutions may present a particular obstacle for effective institutional reform. This raises the question about the likelihood of conflict between indigenous social norms and laws and regulations that are part of market-oriented institutional reform programs. This is the subject of the following section.

3. DIRECT INSTITUTIONAL CONFLICT

So far, we have taken a formal look only at the potential costs and benefits of the implementation of a new law or institutional reform induced by a foreign donor agency. We analysed this in an asymmetric information context between a government (principal) and its implementation agents, combined with a bargaining game regarding implementation and sanctioning between these agents and the constituents. In this section we will be more specific and take a closer look at the substantive aspects of proposed institutional reforms and examine the possible sources of conflict between existing informal institutions, in the context of developing countries and transition economies, and new formal laws, as a function of their typology. In particular, we will look at the general typologies of laws related to the establishment of market economies.

A general perspective on the framing of institutions and the likelihood of conflict

Human action is the consequence of an individual choice among a set of possible actions that individual actors face.[4] Laws split this

---

[4] This set is defined in terms of technological or budgetary feasibility.

set of feasible actions into two subsets of allowed and not allowed actions. This can be done either by prescriptive rules that define the set of allowed actions ('thou shalt do') or proscriptive rules that define the set of not allowed actions ('thou shalt not do') (Coleman, 1990, p.246).

In general, the set of feasible opportunities the actors face is both unknown to the law maker and often infinite. In private societies (*Privatrechtsgesellschaft*) the actors have the right to perform all actions that are not exclusively prohibited by the law: 'If something's not forbidden then it's allowed'. Therefore, rights are usually the consequence of proscriptive laws defining the set of prohibited actions. Duties, by contrast, are in general defined by laws prescribing what kind of actions are to be carried out in what situations. Thus, these laws define a small set of allowed actions. If the number of permitted actions is reduced to one they turn into orders.[5]

In the remainder of this paper, rules that instruct actors to specific actions will be denoted as prescriptive. Rules that just exclude some actions of the set of feasible actions, but leave the actors the autonomy to choose among a variety of remaining actions, will be denoted as proscriptive. Furthermore, the terms prescriptive and proscriptive are used to describe the relative positions of rules within a continuum. The end poles of this continuum are given by rules permitting only one kind of action (i.e. orders) and rules allowing the actors to choose among ∞-1 feasible actions.

The effectiveness of formal institutions
In assessing the effectiveness of laws, it is of crucial relevance to take into account whether they are framed in a prescriptive or proscriptive way. The extent to which rules leave agents a choice among alternative actions determines the likelihood of compatibility

---

[5] Therefore, rules that define what actions the actors have to take are generally framed in a prescriptive way. Proscriptive rules, by contrast, prohibit particular actions while leaving the actors the autonomy to choose among the remaining alternative actions. The extent to which rules leave the actors autonomy depends of course on the number of existent feasible actions (n) and the number of actions prohibited (m). If, for example, $n = 2$ a proscriptive law forbidding one action will have the same constraining effect as a prescriptive rule (Coleman, 1990, p.246). Nevertheless, it is reasonable to assume that in general the existing set of feasible action is infinite. In addition, with a rising number of permitted actions the task of formulating a set of allowed actions instead of the set of prohibited actions becomes quite fast very complex.

between social norms and formal laws, and therefore of compliance with that law.

The efficacy of formal institutions refers to 'the fact that a rule of law which requires certain behaviour is obeyed more often than not' (Hart, 1961, p.100). Thus, laws are effective if in general prescribed actions are carried out and proscribed actions are not and if violations of the law are properly prosecuted and sanctioned (Geiger, 1964, p.68).

With respect to duties, it is quite obvious that laws are effective if the actors usually follow the instructions given. However, with respect to rights, the effectiveness of the underlying proscriptive laws is much harder to determine. Even though the state grants the individual actors rights, it is up to their individual liberty whether they utilise these rights. That is, if the actors voluntarily sacrifice their rights the law is still effective. Take the example of Shasta County, California (Ellickson, 1991), where the law grants that ranchers are not liable for damage caused by stray cattle in open-range areas. Nevertheless, as Ellickson observes in his empirical study, the ranchers usually do provide compensation for damages caused by their cattle because of existing social norms. This leads some authors to conclude that the law is not effective because of these social norms.[6] Such a view, however, ignores the distinction between proscriptive and prescriptive rules.

Prescriptive rules determine what kind of actions the actors are to carry out. Proscriptive rules, by contrast, cannot be carried out. They merely limit the range of permitted actions without determining a particular action (Hayek, 1973/1993, p. 127). Such rules leave the actors the autonomy to choose whatever kind of action they wish, as long as they refrain from taking a prohibited action. If in the Shasta County case the law would have been designed such that the ranchers are not allowed to compensate others, then, indeed, we could conclude that the law would not be effective.[7] However, the actual law does not define a duty, but rather grants a

---

[6] 'Ellickson's study (1991) shows that the farmers of Shasta county, California, in their reciprocal dealings ignored the official property and tort law in favour of rules evolved among themselves. Formally valid law need not be effective.' (Mackaay, 1998, p.31).

[7] Note, that in this case there are only two possible actions (n), to compensate or not to compensate. As pointed out in note 5, if $n = 2$, even a rule defining the set of prohibited actions turns into an order.

right to the ranchers. If the ranchers voluntarily sacrifice this right by delivering compensation it is inappropriate to diagnose an ineffectiveness of the law.[8] Of course, the diagnosis would be different if the actors are illegally forced by other actors not to use their rights. In this case, other proscriptive laws forbidding such action would indeed be violated. The same would be true if additional prescriptive laws exist that define the respective rights as being inalienable (Rose-Ackerman, 1985).

The likelihood of direct conflict between formal and informal institutions
Generally, social norms and laws with contradicting contents are assumed to be inconsistent. However, the argument presented here is that inconsistencies do not necessarily lead to rule violation even if we leave the issue of enforcement aside. Whether inconsistencies with social norms are likely to conflict, i.e. will result in actions violating the law, depends on the degree of prescriptiveness of laws and social norms.

Social norms, like laws, divide the individual choice set into two subsets of allowed and not allowed actions. Inconsistencies arise if the sets of allowed actions under the law and under social norms do not fully overlap. One set will allow more than the other, and conflict may arise. However, the likelihood that such conflict will indeed lead to behaviour violating the law depends on the prescriptiveness (as opposed to proscriptiveness) of the respective laws and social norms. For a particular action *a*, the following combinations (shown in Figure 4.1) are possible. With respect to a particular action, laws and social norms are perfectly consistent for a particular action if it is allowed or not allowed by both law and social norms (upper left and lower right corner of Figure 4.1).

If an action is not allowed by a law, but allowed by a social norm, inconsistency in content arises (lower left corner in Figure 4.1). Yet, with respect to the effectiveness of the law, the question remains whether this inconsistency will indeed lead to actions violating the

---

[8] Of course, information costs may present another reason why actors do not utilise rights granted by the state. However, for law to be effective not all actors have to be lawyers. All they have to know is that they can refer to legal assistance. If this is generally possible there is no reason to assume that laws are ineffective just because the actors do not know their exact content.

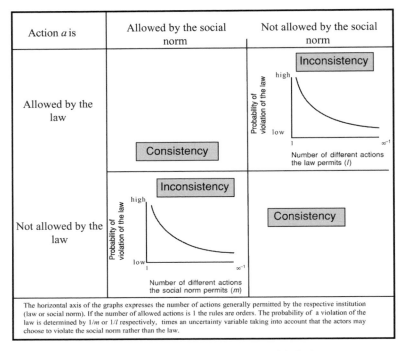

Figure 4.1. Consistency of social norms with the law.

law. If the social norm is proscriptively framed, the particular action is allowed but not commanded. Therefore, the actor is left with the choice of performing other actions instead that will not violate the law. If the social norm, by contrast, is prescriptive the actors are commanded to perform this particular action. Thus, the extent to which such an inconsistency will motivate a violation of the law depends *ceteris paribus* on how prescriptive the social norm is. The more an inconsistent social norm reduces the set of allowed actions, i.e. the more mandatory it is, the higher the probability of a violation of the law.

The second case of inconsistency emerges if an action is allowed by the law, but not by a social norm, i.e. (upper right corner in Figure 4.1). Still, law and social norm may be perfectly compatible with each other, provided that the law allows for this kind of action but does not mandate to perform it. Under this condition, the actors are able to choose another action within the legal frame that makes it possible to comply with both the law and the social norm. If the law, by contrast, prescribes to perform only this particular action the actors are faced with the dilemma of whether to comply with the law or to the contradicting social norm. Thus, it is now the prescriptiveness of the law that raises the probability of a conflicting action. The more a law reduces the set of allowed actions, the higher the probability of a violation of the law, because of contradicting social norms.

Hence, the following propositions can be derived. If the law forbids an action that is allowed by a social norm, the likelihood of conflicting behaviour increases with the prescriptiveness of the social norm. If the law allows an action that is forbidden to be performed by social norms, the likelihood of conflicting behaviour increases with the prescriptiveness of the law.

So far, our analysis allows a general assessment of the extent to which laws are likely to conflict with social norms. It is either the prescriptiveness of the laws and/or that of social norms that leads to a direct conflict in the sense of rule-violating behaviour. In the next section we turn to the more particular case of laws related to the introduction of market-oriented institutional reforms and how they are usually formulated.

The prescriptiveness of formal market institutions

As argued above, a conflicting relationship between formal and informal institutions can be either rooted in the prescriptiveness of formal institutions or in that of social norms. Concentrating in this subsection on the impact of formal institutions, we argue that a direct conflict between formal market institutions and indigenous social norms is principally conceivable only with respect to laws supplementing substantive market laws, but not regarding the institutional core of market systems itself.

Substantive market law
The two pivotal features of economic processes are exchange and competition. Yet, for competition to emerge, first of all exchange

has to take place. As is well known, private actors will only decide to exchange goods or services if the underlying problem of co-operation is sufficiently solved. Because informal institutions, as one possible solution to co-operation problems, destabilise with an increasing number of private actors, societies require accepted laws enforced by a third party. Hence, in line with the argumentation already given by David Hume, a necessary prerequisite for trans-actions on markets are institutions that prohibit the violation of property and contractual obligations and allow for the exchange of property.[9] It is quite obvious that these laws have some cor-respondence to those laws generally identified as the constitutive elements of market economies which are private property, freedom to contract and liability (Furubotn and Richter, 1997, p.11, Kasper and Streit, 1998, p.173). In other words, the constitutive element is the property right per se, but not the degree of its exclusiveness. However, the more exclusive property rights are, the stronger are the incentives for the actors to put them to productive use. The de-gree of universality and exclusiveness of property rights will affect the efficiency with which resources are used (Posner, 1992, p.32). Hence, while the existence of property rights is a necessary require-ment for market transactions to take place, it is their exclusiveness which influences the intensity of market processes. Therefore, in order to understand the impact that institutions present for mar-ket economies we have to distinguish between the 'constituent' function of formal institutions – gained through laws necessary for economic processes – and their 'dynamic' function, which refers to formal institutions influencing the intensity of market processes.

To allow for competition, no further laws are required. If re-sources are scarce competition will be the likely consequence of exchange.[10] The regime of mentioned laws prohibits actors from violating the rights of others in order to succeed in competition. Hence, the substantive law required for the existence of market

---

[9] '[T]he stability of possession, of its transference by consent, and of the performance of promises. 'Tis on the strict observance of those three laws, that the peace and security of human society entirely depend; nor is there any possibility of establishing a good correspondence among men, where these are neglected.' (Hume 1896/1928, p.526.)

[10] What is needed, however, are supplementary laws that protect competition, i.e. that prohibit the collusion of actors within cartels in order to avoid competition. See next section.

economies can be expressed as 'thou shall not violate property rights'. These rules imply a personal liability for contractual obligations and for tortious acts (Alchian, 1977/1965, p.130). Because these institutions merely exclude some actions from the set of allowed actions, they are proscriptive rules. Still, they leave the economic actors a wide open corridor for all kinds of other actions. Therefore, the likelihood of an incompatibility between these laws and social norms is for pure logical reasons quite low.

Law of property

Especially with regard to transition countries that face a tremendous change in property rights structures, a discussion of the impact of market-oriented property law on indigenous social norms is needed. If institutional reforms regulate the distribution of property, it is their prescriptiveness that determines the likelihood of conflict with indigenous social norms. Suppose that some collectively owned resources are allocated to a private actor – a well-known scenario for transition countries, but also for developing countries aiming to fulfil the terms of structural adjustment programmes. In this case, the law grants a right that the actors may voluntary decide not to utilise. If generally accepted social norms exist in this regard, the actor may hand his property right over voluntarily to those who social norms define as the legitimate possessors. This is, for example, what happened in many African countries where, after the assignment of land titles to individuals, the village elders continued to control the allocation of land in their areas (Moore, 1986; Pinckney and Kimuyu, 1994). As long as formal institutions do not define the inalienability of private land titles no laws are violated. The existing social norm will not affect the efficacy of the law granting property rights to specific actors. This would be different only if the law would prescribe that the usage of this particular piece of land is only permitted by the one actor entitled to it.

Supplementary laws and regulations

Laws granting and protecting property rights together with rules determining the distribution of property rights are necessary but insufficient ingredients to constitute market economies. They need to be supplemented by further laws and regulations.[11] First of all, as pointed out, procedural rules and enforcement rules are necessary to let the laws diffuse through the public agencies and make them effective. In addition, laws may be set in order to intervene explicitly in the economic process because of market failure regarding the provision of public goods, or preferences of the constituents for limiting the domain of the market. Thus, regulations for privatised utilities and other monopolies, anti-trust, anti-dumping, financial sector, environment, labour, consumer protection, bankruptcy, etc. will exist. Without enquiring deeply into the legal structure required, it is obvious that to accomplish the respective goals these supplementary regulations usually have to be prescriptively framed. Incompatibilities are therefore quite likely.

To sum up, the more prescriptive laws and regulations are framed, the higher is the likelihood that they will conflict with social norms because of contradictory contents. Therefore, in particular, the generally prescriptive regulatory framework of market economies is likely to conflict with indigenous social norms. The laws of public procurement, for example, are quite prescriptive by defining that it is allowed only to appoint actors according to quality aspects. Hence, in this case an incompatibility with sharing norms of the form 'group members come first' may exist.

The prescriptiveness of social norms and scenarios of direct conflict

It takes two to produce a conflict. This also applies to our analysis of the relationship between formal and informal institutions. Though the proscriptive character of many formal institutions forms a good basis for successful institutional reforms, social norms may still impede the effectiveness of the legal frame.

Prescriptiveness of social norms and the structure of social networks
An inconsistency with substantive market laws arises only if social norms exist that allow for the violation of property rights or that even prescribe actors not to fulfil contracts, to violate private property rights or to harm other actors. Yet, anthropological studies

---

[11] Ellickson classifies these supplementary laws and regulations into remedial rules, procedural rules, constitutive rules and controller-selecting rules (Ellickson, 1991, p.132).

show that – despite many differences in detail – even in traditional societies substantive social norms defining and protecting private property rights exist as well (Goldschmidt, 1951, Popisil, 1958, p.176, Posner, 1980, Benson, 1988, p.774, Kimenyi, 1997, p.13). Correspondingly, these social norms assign liabilities for violating contracts and tortious acts (Malinowski, 1926).[12]

Therefore, what we find in more traditional or less-developed societies is not a principal inconsistency of social norms with the substantive market laws. However, societies exist in which these rules necessary for exchange often do not apply to all members of a society equally, but are restricted to members of comparatively small groups defined by, for example, kinship or tribal origin. This implies that acts violating the property rights of outsiders, i.e. actors not belonging to one's own group, may very well present an action in accordance with the social norms of a group.[13]

Hence, it is the prescriptiveness of social norms governing the behaviour toward outsiders which influences the likelihood that actions conflicting with laws protecting universal property rights may occur (see lower left box in Figure 4.1). If social norms explicitly prescribe violation of property rights of members of other groups, conflict is quite likely. However, if the violation of property rights of outsiders presents only one feasible action among others, such behaviour is less likely to occur. Social fragmentation in a society is a crucial factor. If a society consists of separated groups involved in a continuous fight against each other, social norms are likely to exist that make the violation of property rights of outsiders an obligatory action. In less fragmented societies, social norms may not explicitly demand these kind of actions. And even though groups and social networks exist as well, in less fragmented societies the right of protected property is granted to actors irrespective of their group affiliation. Hence, the effectiveness of the substantive market laws imposed on transition and developing countries is not so much

---

[12] Even in the 'backward society' of Montegrano with its peculiar social norm structure described by Banfield (1958) a 'familism' exists, i.e. groups in which co-operative behaviour takes place.

[13] This is not only an exclusive feature of traditional tribal societies. Examples for such behaviour can be found even in recent history. For example, 'it was considered morally legitimate by Europeans to cheat Native American Indians on the grounds that they were lazy, irrational, and unwilling to repay their debts' (Platteau, 1996, p.770).

endangered by a general inconsistency with social norms existent in these societies. The problem is rather the restriction of these rights to members of one's own group.

So far, we have analysed only pairs of formal and informal institutions in order to find possible inconsistencies which might impede the effectiveness of the respective formal institution. Because private actors are embedded in social networks with a bundle of different norms guiding their behaviour, such an isolated analysis perspective is too narrow. Thus, even if both formal and informal institutions ban the violation of property rights, other norms of the social network might still be the cause of conflicting behaviour.

An example might help clarify this line of thought. Compared to developed economies, in less modern societies property rights are often less universal and less exclusive. Posner (1980) and Ault and Rutman (1979), for example, point out that in primitive law possessory rights on land are common. The property rights, however, are attenuated because the actors are allowed to transfer these rights only to heirs and family members but not to sell them outside the lineage group (Posner, 1980; Cooter, 1991, prescribing the attenuation of individual property rights on land in New Papua New Guinea, and Pinckney and Kimuyu, 1994, in Africa). Institutional reforms standing in contrast to these embedded property rights structures leave individuals with the opportunity to opt for the private right granted by the law and consequently violate the social norm. In this case, they are likely to be punished by those actors who share the respective social norm. However, a conflict in the sense that laws are violated will only occur if these private sanctions do violate individual rights granted by the law (e.g. the right of bodily integrity). Thus, in this case it is not the law imposing private property rights that will be violated, but the substantive market law that prohibits the violation of property rights. Such 'second-order' conflicts between formal and informal institutions, arising because social norms question the exclusive right of the state to sanction, are most likely to be found in fragmented societies with governments lacking the ability to secure individual rights for all members of society equally. Again, we see the important influence the structure of social networks has on possible conflicts between formal and informal institutions.

The impact of legitimacy on the relationship between formal and informal institutions

In our analysis so far, we have implicitly assumed a horizontal relationship between social norms and laws. Yet, even social norms and laws 'which are logically inconsistent in the sense that they may lead in any given situations to requirements or prohibitions of acts of any one person which are mutually contradictory, may yet be made compatible if they stand in a relation of superiority or inferiority to each other, so that the system of rules itself determines which of the rules is to "overrule" the other' (Hayek, 1976/1993, p.24). Thus, even contradictory prescriptive formal and informal institutions can be compatible with each other if corresponding 'collision rules' exist that regulate the application of institutions to different spheres of life. Whether society will subordinate social norms to the law, depends largely on its legitimacy. Legitimacy can reconcile incompatible social norms with the law (Tyler, 1990, p.19).

By legitimacy we do not refer here to any normative convictions concerning the question of whether governments are entitled to rule a society. We use legitimacy as a purely positive concept that describes wide acceptance of the legal force of the government and of the obligatory nature of legal norms (Luhmann, 1969/1993, p.28). It appears that the legitimacy of laws depends less on their overlap with the content of social norms, and more on the way in which laws are established, i.e. the explicit or implicit political con-stitution that regulates how laws are set and changed. It is precisely because of a lack in legitimacy shown in the previous example, that individuals in fear of severe sanctions are forced to cling to social norms on the distribution of property rights despite the fact that formal property rights would benefit them more.

To sum up the main arguments of Section 3, we argued that substantive laws of market economies are not prescriptively but proscriptively framed. Therefore, the likelihood of contradictory contents of social norms is comparatively low, especially compared to the generally prescriptively framed regulations which supplement the substantive laws of market economies. Additionally, studies show that social norms with identical content can be found in all societies. However, with respect to these laws that form the legal core of market economies a conflict may not exist in content but regarding the range of application. Social norms may exist that limit the protection of property rights solely to the members of one's own group. The likelihood that such social norms lead to violations of the substantive market laws depends on their prescriptiveness regarding such behaviour. This in turn is a function of the fragmentation of a society. If the society is highly fragmented social norms may exist prescribing violation of property rights of members of other groups. A lack of legitimacy may prove to be a further hindrance, because conflicting social norms – otherwise being harmless owing to a vertical relationship with formal institutions – compete with formal institutions on a horizontal level.

4. INDIRECT INSTITUTIONAL CONFLICT

Institutional reforms in transition and developing economies do not present an end in themselves. Rather, they are undertaken with the goal of facilitating economic processes and consequently economic growth. However, we have to consider that social norms may not lead to violations of these laws, yet may seriously impede economic growth. As already mentioned, institutions generally serve two purposes regarding market processes. They allow processes to take place (constituent function) and they influence the quality of market processes (dynamic function). As we have already analysed the impact of informal institutions on the constituent function of formal institutions by looking for possible rule-violations due to their existence, this section focuses on indirect conflicts due to social norms impeding economic growth.

The economic efficiency of social norms is a controversial issue. Even though we can derive many arguments for why existing social norms might be 'inefficient' (Elster, 1989, Posner, 1996a), there is no convincing way to prove this assertion as soon as we leave the neo-classical, zero-transaction world. 'Seek and ye shall find' can always be used as an argument for why any real world situation may be an efficient response to transaction costs (Furubotn and Richter, 1997). Even comparative analysis (Demsetz, 1969) does not allow escape from this problem, because firstly, it is difficult to identify and assess all relevant characteristics of norms, secondly, the number of variants that can be taken into account may be too small and thirdly, static and dynamic analysis may deliver inconsistent results (Furubotn and Richter, 1997, p.475). Furthermore, economic efficiency can be assessed only with respect to the outcomes that individual actors pursue. Non-economic motives and 'passions', are likely to play an important role in social norms (see Posner, 1996b, 1720).

The concept of market compatibility

Because of these flaws of applying the concept of efficiency to norms, we propose a different yardstick in order to grasp the economic impact of social norms. Exchange and competition present the two central features of market processes. While exchange forms the very basis of markets, the intensity of competition affects the rate of innovation and thus determines the dynamics of market processes. Metaphorically speaking, exchange presents the engine that allows for economic growth and competition the accelerator that determines its speed.

Therefore, in order to assess the impact of social norms on market processes we scrutinise their impact on exchange and the intensity of competition. Analysing this 'market compatibility' of social norms avoids the problems that are involved with the concept of efficiency.[14] Firstly, we do not have to consider all characteristics

---

[14] The concept of 'market compatibility' refers to the working properties of the spontaneous market order. It has been developed within the German Freiburg School of Economics in order to assess the impact of policy interventions into the market. Wilhelm Röpke, for example, defines interventions into the economic process as compatible if they 'do not interfere with the price mechanism and with the automatism of the market derived from it' (Röpke, 1950, p.160, for an extensive discussion see also Thalheim, 1955, Tuchtfeldt, 1960). However, due to transaction costs the price mechanism is not the only information generating device affecting the allocation of resources. It is supplemented by networks which allow for important non-price signals like reputation (Granovetter, 1985). Thus, non-interference with the price mechanism may not present a proper yardstick for market

of social norms, but can limit our analysis to their impact on exchange and competition. Secondly, we do not have to refer to any comparative analysis. Thirdly, by focusing on competition we take a dynamic view and fourthly, we do not have to take into account what kind of ends the actors pursue, since we concentrate only on the impact of a social norm on economic growth regardless of the actors' position toward competition and exchange.

The existence of generally shared norms that exclude the violation of property rights of actors is a necessary prerequisite for transactions to take place. Beside these necessary social norms, we can distinguish between social norms that are supporting and restraining market processes.[15]

Social norms such as private dispute-resolving mechanisms or, in particular, commercial norms, back up market transactions (Bernstein, 1996). By reducing transaction costs they facilitate and thus support market processes. An example for social norms enhancing the intensity of competition would be norms favouring a competitive attitude. Social norms restrain market processes if they imply behaviour that has an inhibiting effect on the dynamics of the market process. They can be directed at transactions, e.g. social norms that restrict exchange to non-pecuniary items or social norms against taking interest for lending money, or have a dampening effect on the intensity of competition, e.g. social norms that forbid individual actors to strive for economic gains entirely.[16]

---

compatibility. Instead we will concentrate on the central features of market processes which are exchange and competition (Wegner, 1997, p.505).

[15] Of course, there are as well many social norms that have no impact on the dynamics of the market process. Such neutral social norms will not be of consideration in the following analysis.

[16] Traditional sharing norms are often considered as restraining market processes. However, whether they are restraining or rather supporting depends on the respective circumstances. In traditional societies characterised by high dependence on an unstable environment, they tend to stabilise economic interaction by reducing individual risks (Platteau, 1996, p.11, Collier and Gunning, 1999, p.78). Thus, they actually support market transaction under these circumstances. Therefore, in order to assess the market compatibility of social norms it is necessary to take the respective circumstances into account. If no effective legal structure is existing such traditional norms may present solutions that allow at least for minimal economic activities to take place. But with an effective legal structure traditional sharing norms may by reducing incentives for economic activities very well restrain market processes.

*The impact of restraining social norms in combination
with fragmented societies*

Our differentiation is based on the effect social norms have on exchange in general and on the intensity of competition. It is their normative content with respect to particular actions that decides whether they support or restrain market processes.[17] In societies with social norms that do not score highly in terms of market compatibility, we will observe a low intensity of impersonal exchange and competition and consequently the complete absence of, or only very little, economic growth. However, the content of social norms is just one of two determinants.

While it is the content of social norms that determines the direction of their impact on economic processes, it is the number of actors to whom the norms apply that determines the intensity of the respective effects. Which actors do fall under the shelter of a social norm depends on the entry barriers of a group, the features that individual actors should have in order to fall under the jurisdiction of a social norm. Social norms can refer solely to actors defined by kinship or tribal origin, they can refer only to actors defined by function, e.g. traders in the same area of business, or they can refer to all actors equally. While the entry barriers are high in the former case, they are nil in the latter.

If necessary and supporting norms are restricted solely to the immediate members of one's own group, then the positive impact on economic processes will be comparatively low. Economic processes will take place only within groups defined by social features like kinship or tribal origin, but not between members of different groups. If, by contrast, these norms apply equally to all individual actors of a society, market exchange can take place on a much larger scale. Correspondingly, the dynamics of the market processes will be much stronger. The positive impact of these social norms depends crucially on the criteria actors have to fulfil in order to belong under the umbrella of these norms. The lower the entry barriers to

---

[17] To avoid misunderstanding, it does not hold that only proscriptive norms support market processes while prescriptive social norms restrain these processes. For example, the norms of a protestant ethic are quite prescriptive (Weber, 1905/1993). Nevertheless, these norms clearly support economic processes.

groups, the more these social norms support the dynamics of the market process.

This is different for restraining social norms. In this case, the intensity of the negative impact of such informal institutions depends on how easily actors can escape from them. If the exit costs, that is, the costs incurred by leaving the respective group or social network, are low, the negative impact of restraining norms will be comparatively weak. But to exit a group may become very costly for an actor. This is in particular true for groups (primarily defined by kinship) in subsistence societies, in which informal institutions provide crucial economic functions. They solve agency problems in transactions and reduce social risks: 'the extended family system serves as an insurance fund, as an informal poor law, as a means for pooling and circulating capital within a group, and also as an outlet for charity and generosity' (Bauer and Yamey, 1957, p.65). The consequences of exit from one without the opportunity of entry into other social networks are described by Marris and Somerset in an empirical analysis of Kenyan entrepreneurs: 'He is therefore doubly isolated, both within his community and the wider society, withdrawing from the one to meet the demands of the other, and belonging to neither. This insecurity drives him back on a mistrustful, self-reliant style of management . . . The growth of his business is constrained by the limits of what he can personally supervise . . .' (Marris and Somerset, 1971, p.227). Exit usually requires the option of entry to another group. The lower exit and entry barriers are, the weaker will be the negative impact of restraining social norms on economic processes.

Therefore, the entry barriers to groups crucially determine the intensity of the impact of social norms on economic processes. In fragmented societies the positive impact of supporting norms will be comparatively weak while the negative impact of restraining norms will be strong. Again it turns out that the fragmentation of a society presents a central variable (shown in Figure 4.2). Therefore, even if market-oriented institutional reforms are perfectly implemented, economic growth may not show up at all or only very minimally. Thus, the long-term and less directly visible benefits of market-oriented institutional reforms require even more time to show up. Consequently, since the effect of the reform will not meet the hopes

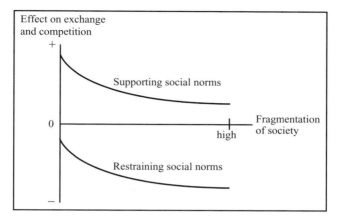

Figure 4.2. Impact of social fragmentation on economic processes.

of the government as well as the citizens that had opted for reforms in the first place, resistance may grow and eventually lead to a withdrawal of the institutional reform.

Now that the potential conflicts that social norms could present *vis-à-vis* the implementation of market-oriented reforms have been analysed, a last important question remains to be answered. Obviously, the best solution to these implementation problems would be if social norms impeding the effectiveness of formal institutions and restraining market processes would vanish in the course of reform. But is this solution likely to occur? Moreover, under what conditions can we expect social norms to erode? Thus, before we turn to the implications of our analysis, we will scrutinise in the following section what determines the stability of such social norms.

5. THE STABILITY OF INFORMAL INSTITUTIONS

Factors influencing social norms to change

Social norms do adapt to changes in the environment. However, in reality we find examples of both very slow (e.g. the social norm of duelling, Posner, 1996a) and very rapid change (e.g. social norms against cohabitation of unmarried couples, Bikhchandani, *et al.*, 1992). In economics, the emergence and change of social norms is usually modelled as diffusion processes characterised by critical masses allowing for multiple equilibria to occur (Akerlof, 1980; Romer, 1984; Witt, 1989; Bikhchandani *et al.*, 1992; Cooter, 1997; Kuran, 1998; Witt, 1999). Nevertheless, even in the face of multiple possible equilibria, such an approach allows identification of the conditions that determine the pace at which social norms are likely to change.

The central element of these models is that individual actors choose their actions under the influence of social constraints that they themselves create and sustain. These models are based on two central assumptions. Firstly, the individual decision of whether to comply with a social norm is driven by opportunity costs. Secondly, network effects crucially affect the stability of social norms. In the model that we developed in Section 2, social norms were considered exogenous. The costs of compliance were calculated for government agents and constituents. In this section, social norms will be endogenised and allowed to change, as a function of the number of constituents and the distribution of compliance cost–benefit ratios in a group.

An actor will comply with a social norm as long as the discounted utility he expects to realise from compliance will exceed the discounted utility he expects to derive from violating this norm, i.e. $U^{SN} - U^{NSN} > 0$. The difference $(U^{SN} - U^{NSN})$ expresses the net benefit an individual actor derives from following a social norm. Similar to Posner (1996a) we will denote this net utility as the compliance–noncompliance differential with respect to a social norm.[18] It is the difference between the respective payoffs and not their absolute size that determines first the compliance to a social norm and second the stability of such compliance in consequence of exogenous changes. Even if the payoffs from complying to a social norm decline for whatever reasons, as long as the payoff from violating the social norm declines more rapidly, the actor will continue to comply to it (Posner, 1996a, 142).

---

[18] Posner (1996a) denotes these net-opportunity costs as co-operation-defection differential. He focuses on the general stability of groups. However, we are not so much interested in the erosion of groups but in the erosion of social norms existing within one group. Despite the erosion of one social norm the group may continue to exist.

According to the assumption of individual expected utility maximisation, the stability of a social norm depends on the development of the payoffs an actor can realise by either action–compliance or non-compliance – over time. These payoffs are the result of both endogenous and exogenous processes. However, the net utility an actor can draw from complying with or violating a social norm depends on the intensity of network effects.

Many social norms can be interpreted as solutions to problems of strategic interaction within a group. Social norms present solutions to problems of co-ordination such as defining the rules of traffic or language. Furthermore, social norms exist as solutions to problems of co-operation and help to overcome inefficient Nash-equilibria. Social norms that enforce the mutual recognition of property rights and thus allow for Pareto improvements have been discussed above. In general, the utility an actor derives from complying with a social norm depends on the share of actors that comply to the social norm as well, $U^{SN} = \phi(n - \tilde{n}/n)$, with $\tilde{n}$ denoting the number of group members that violate the social norm and some monotonous function ϕ that expresses the intensity of the network effect, that is the interdependency between the actors. The number of actors necessary to make $U^{SN} > U^{NSN}$ – the critical mass – will be denoted as n^*.

While conventions are self enforcing, this does not hold for social norms that present solutions to problems of co-operation. These norms require an enforcement mechanism by which defecting group members will be punished. The threat of sanctions changes the individual payoffs in a way that turns cooperation into the dominant strategy (Ullman-Margalit, 1978, Frank, 1988).[19] Thus, the utility an actor assigns to an action violating a social norm depends on how fiercely other group members will sanction such violations. Therefore, the gross utility that an actor assigns to an action a_j that will violate a social norm ($a_j \notin A^A_{SN}$) has to be reduced by the cost imposed on him via sanctions by his fellow group members times the probability that his action will be observed,

---

[19] With respect to informal sanctioning a co-operation problem exists itself. Thus, we are faced with a second order dilemma. The assumption that those actors who will not sanction deviant behaviour will themselves be imposed to sanctions leads to an infinite chain of reasoning. However, since we do not intend to analyse in this paper how such norms may emerge, we will not tackle this issue.

i.e. $U^{NSN} = U(a_j) - \rho C.$[20] The extent of sanctions he will have to suffer depends on the share of group members that are willing to sanction him. In general, the higher the share of norm followers, the higher will be the sanction a deviator would have to suffer for violating this rule. Hence, we assume that C is determined by both the share of norm compliers and the strength of interdependency $C = \phi(n - \tilde{n}/n)$.

It follows from these assumptions that the stability of a social norm depends on how exogenous changes will affect the individual compliance–non-compliance differentials and on the endogenous repercussion on social norms that such changes will induce.

In the trivial case exogenous events may change the utility of either or both behavioural options in a way that turns the compliance–non-compliance differential negative for all actors. Thus, the larger the original compliance–non-compliance differentials of the individual actors are, the less likely it is that external changes will be able to undermine a social norm (Posner, 1996a, p.141).

While for homogenous groups it is only the value of the compliance–non-compliance differential that decides about the stability of a social norm, for heterogeneous groups the composition of the group matters as well. If some actors face such a small positive compliance–non-compliance differential that exogenous changes are sufficient to turn it negative, the relative frequency of social norm compliance within the group will decrease. Because of the interdependency of the actors, such individual action will create network externalities. These changes in the frequency of norm compliance will decrease U^{SN} and increase U^{NSN} for all other actors. Consequently, the size of the compliance–non-compliance

[20] Furthermore, the utility the actor assigns to an action a_j is affected by the specificness of his hitherto taken investments that would be rendered invalid by dismissing the social norm. Actors have to incur costs in order to learn the content of norms and to develop corresponding routines, i.e. they have to invest in their human capital. Furthermore, actors may have gained knowledge which can serve them to improve in exercising activities which are the result of the incentive structure of the social norm. To the extent that these investments in human capital cannot be used after violating the social norm, they are specific. The same applies if the individual actors invest in material assets to perform certain activities in response to the incentive structure of the existing norms. To the extent that these assets cannot be utilised after violating the social norm, they are specific as well.

differentials of the remaining actors diminishes. Again, the question is whether these repercussions will be sufficient to turn the compliance–non-compliance differential negative and by this initiate a propagation process that leads to a norm erosion. The likelihood that such cascades will occur depends on different factors and multiple equilibria are possible.

The intensity of network effects presents one of these factors. If the individual utilities are highly dependent on each other, small variations of n are likely to lead to an erosion of the norm. However, as ϕ affects both U^{SN} and U^{NSN}, yet in opposite directions, exogenous shocks either have to be quite strong in order to affect the compliance–non-compliance differential sufficiently to turn it negative or the original compliance–non-compliance differential of some actors has to be at the margin. Therefore, the distribution of the individual differentials presents another and even more crucial factor. The greater the number of actors whose differentials will be turned negative by the initial exogenous change, the stronger will be the impact on the differential of the other group members. Thus, the lower the average compliance–non-compliance differential is and, in the case of heterogeneous actors, the more left skewed the distribution of the individual differentials is, the higher are the chances that small shocks will lead to a fast erosion of a social norm. Ensminger (1992) describes how economic changes led to a dramatically increased diversity among the Kenyan Orma and then resulted in a change of social norms. While some actors became commercial producers, traders, farmers, and wage labourers, others remained in subsistence pastoral production. As a consequence, divergent interest regarding the appropriate form of property rights emerged and induced institutional change.

So far, we have discussed the propagation processes that may be initiated if, owing to an exogenous shock for a given compliance level, U^{NSN} rises above U^{SN} for some or even all actors. However, even if at the original level of compliance ($\hat{n} > n^*$) the differentials remain positive for all actors norm erosion may occur. This may take place if, as a result of exogenous changes, it happens that $(U^{NSN} \mid n < n^*) > (U^{NSN} \mid \hat{n})$. If the actors would be much better off with an activity that is forbidden by a social norm, if this norm no longer exists this may elicit some form of collective action. If a privileged group is concerned, it may happen that one or just some actors are actively attempting to initiate a process of norm erosion. All that these agents have to achieve is to induce a sufficient number of other agents to expect that collective aversion will come about, so that the expectation becomes self-fulfilling (Witt, 1989, 166).

Destabilising effects of formal institutions on social norms

After discussing the basic features and dynamics of economic models of social norms, we will now turn to the effects laws have on social norms. Posner (1996a) argues that laws affect the value of compliance–non-compliance differential directly if they either subsidise or punish social norm activities. Furthermore, he points out that by affecting the individual differentials they may have an indirect effect on the stability of social norms.

We like to supplement this argument by proposing that in particular those legal changes that are necessary to constitute market economies create even more pervasive effects on the stability of social norms. A coherent and complete introduction of laws constituting a market economy will tend to destabilise restraining social norms. They open up entrepreneurial opportunities: and because the inclination to take risks and to innovate is usually not uniformly distributed, such laws will create heterogeneity within so far homogenous groups by increasing U^{NSN} for entrepreneurial actors. Thus, the introduction of a low transaction cost legal frame of market economies increases the likelihood that the compliance–non-compliance differentials of actors will decrease sufficiently to make them violate the social norm or even attempt to intentionally induce a process of social norm erosion. Moreover, entrepreneurial activities by some actors will increase the intensity of competition for scarce resources and by this will tend to further reduce U^{SN} comparatively to U^{NSN} over time. Thus, it will become increasingly beneficial to transact with outsiders as well. Consequently, a self-propelling process of decreasing fragmentation and the erosion of restraining social norms may take place.

Economic history provides ample evidence for such processes. The importance of entrepreneurs violating the traditional social norms of their groups and by this initiating a process of change is in particular emphasised by Hayek in order to explain the emergence of growing market economies in Western Europe:

There can be little doubt that from the toleration of bartering with outsiders, the recognition of delimited private property, especially in land, the enforcement of contractual obligations, the competition with fellow craftsmen in the same trade, the variability of initially customary prices, the lending of money, particularly at interest, were all initially infringements of customary rules – so many falls from grace. And the law-breakers, who were to be path-breakers, certainly did not introduce the new rules because they recognised that they were beneficial to the community, but they simply started some practices advantageous to them which then did prove beneficial'. (Hayek, 1979/1993, p.161)

Whereas the process of institutional change underlying economic development in Western Europe described by Hayek emerged endogenously, the institutional change being of interest in the present paper is exogenously induced by market-oriented institutional reforms. But if the legal foundations of a market economy that are needed in order to destabilise conflicting and restraining social norms have to be implemented by public agents which are themselve embedded in the problematic socio-economic environment, we do face a kind of lock-in situation. The destabilising effect will only occur under the condition that the substantive market laws as well as supplementary regulations are effective and that the actors can refer to these laws at low costs.

Transacting with actors not belonging to one's own group is less risky in a world with an adequate legal framework than in one without it. Even though most disputes in economic transactions are solved by social norms, the law and its enforcement by the state provides an 'enforcement of last resort'. The law provides the actors with legal 'weapons' which they may or may not use. Thus, the law determines the threat points in the process of individual bargaining over contract fulfilment or other disputes to which each party can resort (Baird *et al.*, 1994, ch. 7). By this, laws do not only help to back up the transactions within networks, they also reduce the uncertainty involved in transactions with outsiders. By reducing the costs of transacting with new counterparts an effective legal framework reduces both the entry barriers into networks and the costs of establishing new ones. Additionally, such laws reduce the exit barriers of groups by defining and protecting individual rights that other group members are not allowed to violate.

Legal deficiencies (e.g. corruption in bureaucracies or laws and regulations being changed frequently in unpredictable ways) in contrast raise the dependency of individuals with regard to their social networks, especially if the traditional social networks also offer insurance against risks of ageing and illness. In all these cases the consequence will be high transaction costs for the actors. Therefore, although a legal frame exists *de jure*, the actors still may be better off if they continue to refer to the (comparatively cost free) social norms within their traditional groups. De Soto (1989) provides a striking example of how high costs of using the state law apparatus force economic actors to turn to private solutions to their problems. If the quality of the legal structure is very poor, that is if laws are not complete, 'clear, widely known, coherent, applicable to all, predictable, credible and properly and evenly enforced' (Burki and Perry, 1998) reliance on the social norms that exist within the traditional, well-defined groups defined by ethnicity or kinship represents a rational strategy.

6. SUMMARY AND POLICY IMPLICATIONS

This chapter has focused on the 'embeddedness' of institutional reforms in the wider socio-economic environment of the recipient country. We have analysed the conflicting potential indigenous social norms may present if – as is the case with externally induced institutional reforms – new legislation does not build upon the social structures which have grown over years in the recipient country and probably present responses to very specific environmental conditions.

The good news on this matter is:

(a) Unless we have an extreme case of societal fragmentation, with regard to substantive market laws a direct conflict between formal and informal institutions leading to rule-violating behaviour is unlikely to occur. The proscriptive character of laws constituting market economies leaves the actors with a wide spectrum of different actions to choose at hand. Therefore, even if social norms happen to be framed in a more prescriptive way, the result of their relationship with substantive market laws will seldom impede the effectiveness of these formal institutions.

(b) In addition, contradictions between formal and informal institutions regarding their content do not necessarily lead to rule-violations by private actors. As long as the members of a society are willing to subordinate social norms to the laws and accept the fact that these different institutions apply to different spheres of life (e.g. public and private life), implementation problems will be rare.

(c) Another promising result of our analysis is, that, with regard to the stability of social norms, a coherent and complete introduction of laws constituting a market economy will tend to destabilise social norms which, in principle, undermine the effectiveness of formal institutions (direct conflict) or the dynamic of market processes (indirect conflict).

Unfortunately, there is also bad news:

(a) First of all, the legal foundation of market economies consists not only of substantive market laws, but also of supplementary laws and regulations, which are generally framed prescriptively. Hence, with respect to those formal institutions prescriptive social norms may indeed pose a threat to their effectiveness.

(b) Such direct conflicts between supplementary laws and regulations and social norms will have negative repercussions. The substantive market laws will only be effective if the supplementary laws and regulations are followed by the executive and judiciary body.

(c) A further consequence is that in this course of action the effects on the compliance–non-compliance differential regarding 'problematic' social norms will probably not be high enough to induce a collective aversion and, subsequently, an erosion of the social norm.

(d) Besides direct conflicts, social norms may also restrain the dynamic of market processes. This presents a problem for implementing institutional reforms in the sense that the hope for a 'better world' comparable to the achievements of industrialised nations is for many people in the recipient countries the main reason for accepting institutional change in the first place. As soon as this hope vanishes, social unrest especially regarding the distribution of resources is likely to occur.

(e) Finally, we have argued that the extent of direct and indirect conflicts between formal and informal institutions depends largely on the structure of society: fragmented societies show severe insider–outsider differentiations. Thus, the probability of prescriptive social norms even contradicting substantive market laws regarding their universal application of rights and duties is higher. Also, the willingness to bring social norms into a vertical relationship to formal institutions is rather low, owing to deficits with respect to legitimacy and, subsequently, deficits regarding an explicit or at least implicit consensus about the rights and obligations of both the government and the citizens irrespective of which actors currently form the government (Holcombe, 1994, p.41).[21]

Now, how should we handle these? Because the structure of society plays such an important role for the success of institutional reforms, a profound diagnosis of the concrete social structure – the degree of general consensus reached in society, the openness of social networks etc. – is needed. The degree to which the problem of co-operation within the larger context of a society is solved has been increasingly approached under the heading of social capital (Coleman, 1990, Ostrom, 1990, Putnam, 1993, La Porta *et al.*, 1997). Social capital refers to the existence of generalised trust and informal institutions that prevent opportunism in interactions even with actors of other networks. The emergence of social capital can only be realised through ongoing interaction. This is less likely if a society is split up into separated groups.[22] There is empirical

---

[21] Collier and Dollar find that in democratic political systems the negative impact of ethnic diversion on growth vanishes (Collier and Gunning, 1999, p.67). However, the question is whether democratic political institutions help to heal the negative consequences of ethnic division, or whether healed ethnic division, i.e. co-operation between the different ethnic groups of a society, allows for democracy.

[22] Thus, the reason why even after independence the laws in many African states were not perceived as legitimate is a lack of social consensus: 'The nationalist movement was essentially a coalition of disparate groups united by their common grievances against colonial oppression . . . Although the members of the coalition fought against the colonial power, they worried about the enormous power they were trying to wrestle from it, power they could not entrust to any one of them or even share in a way that could reduce political anxiety' (Ake, 1996, p.4). After independence it came increasingly to a 'conflict among nationalities, ethnic groups, and communal and interest groups' (Ake, 1996, p.5).

evidence that ethnic fragmentation in particular appears to be negatively related to the existence of political institutions and the provision of public goods (Easterly and Levine, 1997, Temple and Johnson, 1998).[23]

In order to 'measure' social capital, i.e. co-operation on the intergroup level, Knack and Keefer (1997) as well as La Porta *et al.* (1997) draw on data from the World Values Surveys (1994). Putnam (1993) utilises other variables in order to measure social capital of which, in particular, the participation in horizontally organised associations (e.g. sports clubs, social associations, music bands) has become popular in the literature.[24] However, Knack and Keefer (1997) find no correlation between associational activity and economic performance.[25]

In searching for possible conflicting social norms the compliance–non-compliance differential presented in Section 5 might be helpful. It makes a difference to the planning institutional reforms to know whether possible conflicting norms are already on the edge of erosion (compliance–non-compliance differential close to zero) or in such a 'comfortable' position that even tremendous changes in the environment will not affect them substantially.

In order to avoid a conflict some authors propose to shape the law in line with social norms (Dia, 1996, Cooter, 1997, Voigt and Kiwit, 1998). However, aligning social norms with the law is a reasonable option for only a limited number of formal institutions. Obviously and quite self evidently, aligning substantive market laws to conflicting social norms is out of the question. The

---

[23] This corresponds with empirical studies that find a negative correlation between ethnic fragmentation and successful policy reforms (Dollar and Svensson, 1998) and studies pointing to a negative correlation between ethnic heterogeneity and economic growth (Adelman and Morris, 1967, Haug, 1967, Reynolds, 1985).

[24] Actually he uses three more indicators: newspaper readership, referenda turnout and the extent to which voters have exercised preference votes in elections, that is the voters indicate on the ballot paper not only the party they vote for but also that they prefer a particular candidate from the party list they have chosen even though it is not required to make the vote count (Putnam, 1993, p.91).

[25] Associations obviously can have both positive and negative effects. If they are open to members of different groups they may, as Putnam argues, support intergroup cooperation. This is different if associations are confined to members of one particular group. Furthermore, while associations may increase general co-operation, at the same time they may lead to economic cartels or rent-seeking lobbies (Olson, 1982). Consequently Knack and Keefer (1997) try to distinguish between 'Putnam-Groups' and 'Olson-Groups'. The results, however, remain unclear as it may not be possible to distinguish convincingly between socially efficient and inefficient groups (Knack and Keefer, 1997, pp.1274).

whole reform purpose would be perverted. Only with respect to social norms having a constituent function for market processes and/or supporting market processes might an alignment be sensible. Cooter correctly acknowledges that the appeal for alignment of social norms with the law is the strongest for business norms that evolve in a system of open competition, yet the weakest with respect to oppressive social norms such as the suppression of women or the practice of blood feuds (Cooter, 1997, p.208). With particular regard to developing countries, Dia (1996) comes to a similar conclusion. He proposes as well to reconcile laws and social norms, yet limits his recommendation to those social norms that 'are open to modern technology and challenges (renovation)' (Dia, 1996, p.29).

The embeddedness of the public agents in social networks may present a major obstacle to the efficacy of implanted formal institutions. The options to solve the agency problems with respect to the public agents are limited. Compensation schemes that would minimise agency costs often cannot be afforded and would be useless in the face of powerful social networks. Thus, in order to make implementation more likely it may be necessary to isolate the public agent from the social networks. This can be done by introducing external public agents. For example, civil rights for black Americans in the south of the United States were implemented with the help of federal authorities and agents external to this region. Another option is to replace a spoils system by new agents. This measure has been followed, for example, in the republic of Georgia. In order to increase the effectiveness of the new civil law all judges were required to pass a written exam on the new law. Those who failed had to leave office. By this, more than 50% of the judges were replaced and it has been ensured that the jurisdiction is well informed on the new laws.

As already mentioned, rule-violating behaviour by private actors can be reduced if the dependency on traditional social networks is lowered. A possible means of breaking up social ties born out of a lack of alternatives is precisely to offer alternatives. If private actors are able, for example, to take insurances against illness and ageing or can lend money at reasonable interest rates, reasons for engaging in costly risk-diverging strategies guided mainly through social norms of the extended family may vanish.

Of course, if societies are highly fragmented, we do face severe problems of embedding externally induced institutional reforms. The option of implementation by external agents financed through external capital may be the only promising approach left. An example is provided by the situation in Kosovo, where the law is enforced by public agents provided by the United Nations. The societal division in former Yugoslavia presents the extreme case where the barriers for effective market-oriented institutional reforms are very high. In other less pathological cases, a combination of the different policy options presented here may help to increase the efficacy of the implanted laws.

REFERENCES

Adelman, Irma and Morris, Cynthia Taft (1967) *Society, Politics, and Economic Development*. Baltimore: Johns Hopkins University Press.

Ake, Claude (1996) *Democracy and Development in Africa*. Washington DC: The Brookings Institution.

Akerlof, George A. (1980) A theory of social custom, of which unemployment may be one consequence. *Quarterly Journal of Economics*, 94, 749–775.

Alchian, Armen A. (1977/1965) Some economics of property rights. *Il Politico, 30, 816–29*. Reprinted in: *Economic Forces at Work*. pp. 127–149. Indianapolis: Liberty Fund.

Aoki, Masahiko (1998) *The Subjective Game Form and Institutional Evolution as Punctuated Equilibrium*. Lecture at the Paris Conference of the International Society for New Institutional Economics.

Ault, David E. and Rutman, Gilbert L. (1979) The development of individual rights to property in tribal Africa. *Journal of Law and Economics*, 22(1), 163–182.

Baird, Douglas G., Gertner, Robert H., and Picker, Randal C. (1994) *Game Theory and the Law*. Cambridge, MA: Harvard University Press.

Banfield, Edward C. (1958) *The Moral Basis of a Backward Society*. Chicago: The Free Press.

Bardach, Eugene (1977) *The Implementation Game: What Happens After a Bill Becomes A Law*. Cambridge, MA: The MIT Press.

Bauer, Peter T. and Yamey B.S. (1957) *The Economics of Under-Developed Countries*. Cambridge: Cambridge University Press.

Benson, Bruce L. (1988) Legal evolution in primitive societies. *Journal of Institutional and Theoretical Economics*, 144 (5), 772–788.

Bernstein, Lisa (1996) Merchant law in a merchant court: rethinking the code's search for immanent business norms. *University of Pennsylvania Law Review*, 144, 1765–1821.

Bikhchandani, S., Hirshleifer, David and Welch, Ivo (1992) A theory of fads, fashion, custom, and cultural changes as informational cascades. *Journal of Political Economy*, 100 (5), 992–1026.

Buchanan, James M. (1975) *The Limits of Liberty – Between Anarchy and Leviathan.* Chicago: University of Chicago Press.

Burki, Shahid Javed and Perry, Guillermo E. (1998) *Beyond the Washington Consensus: Institutions Matter.* Washington DC: The World Bank.

Coleman, James S. (1990) *Foundations of Social Theory.* Cambridge, MA: The Belknap Press of Harvard University Press.

Collier, Paul and Gunning, Jan William (1999) Explaining African economic performance. *Journal of Economic Literature*, XXXVII (1), 64–111.

Cooter, Robert D. (1991) Inventing market property: the land courts of Papua New Guinea. *Law & Society Review*, 25(4).

(1997) The rule of state law and the rule-of-law state: economic analysis of the legal foundations of development. In: Bruno, M. and Pleskovic, B. (eds.) *Annual World Bank Conference on Development Economics 1996.* pp. 191–217. Washington DC: The World Bank.

De Soto, Hernandez (1989) *The Other Path. The Invisible Revolution in the Third World.* New York: Harper and Row.

Demsetz, Harold (1969) Information and efficiency: another viewpoint. *Journal of Law and Economics*, 12, 1–22.

Dia, Mamadou (1996) *Africa's Management in the 1990s and Beyond. Reconciling Indigenous and Transplanted Institutions.* Washington, DC: The World Bank.

Dollar, David and Svensson, Jakob (1998) *What Explains the Success or Failure of Structural Adjustment Programs? World Bank Working Paper Series.* Washington DC: World Bank.

Downs, Anthony (1967/1994) *Inside Bureaucracy.* Prospect Heights: Waveland Press.

Easterly, William and Levine, Ross (1997) Africa's growth tragedy: policies and ethnic divisions. *Quarterly Journal of Economics*, 112 (4), 1203–1250.

Ellickson, Robert C. (1991) *Order without Law. How Neighbors Settle Disputes.* Cambridge, MA: Harvard University Press.

Elster, Jon (1989) *The Cement of Society.* Cambridge: Cambridge University Press.

Ensminger, Jean (1992) *Making a Market: The Institutional Transformation of an African Society.* Cambridge: Cambridge University Press.

Frank, Robert H. (1988) *Passions Within Reason – The Strategic Role of Emotions.* New York: W.W. Norton & Company.

Furubotn, Eirik G. and Richter, Rudolf (1997) *Institutions and Economic Theory. The Contribution of the New Institutional Economics.* Ann Arbor: University of Michigan Press.

Geiger, Theodor (1964) *Vorstudien zu einer Soziologie des Rechts.* Neuwied: Luchterhand.

Goldschmidt, W. (1951) Ethics and the Structure of Society: an Ethnological Contribution to the Sociology of Knowledge. *American Anthropologist*, 53, 506–524.

Granovetter, Mark (1985) Economic action, social structure, and embeddedness. *American Journal of Sociology*, 91, 481–510.

Hart, Herbert Lionel Adolphus (1961) *The Concept of Law.* London: Oxford University Press.

Haug, Marie R. (1967) Social and cultural pluralism as a concept in social system analysis. *American Journal of Sociology*, 73, 294–304.

Hayek, Friedrich August (1973/1993): *Law, Legislation and Liberty. Volume 1 Rules and Order.* Padstow: T. J. Press Ltd.

   (1976/1993): *Law, Legislation and Liberty. Volume 2 The Mirage of Social Justice.* Padstow: T. J. Press Ltd.

   (1979/1993): *Law, Legislation and Liberty. Volume 3 The Political Order of a Free People.* Padstow: T. J. Press Ltd.

Holcombe, Randall G. (1994) *The Economic Foundations of Government.* New York: New York University Press.

Hume, David (1896/1928) *A Treatise of Human Nature.* Oxford: Clarendon Press.

Kasper, Wolfgang and Streit, Manfred E. (1998) *Institutional Economics. Social Order and Public Policy.* Cheltenham: Edward Elgar.

Kimenyi, Mwangi S. (1997) *Ethnic Diversity, Liberty and the State.* Cheltenham: Edward Elgar.

Knack, Stephen and Keefer, Philip (1997) Does social capital have an economic payoff? A cross-country investigation. *Quarterly Journal of Economics*, 112 (4), 1251–1288.

Knight, Jack (1992) *Institutions and Social Conflict.* Cambridge: Cambridge University Press.

Kuran, Timur (1998) Ethnic norms and their transformation through reputational cascades. *Journal of Legal Studies*, XXVII, 623–659.

La Porta, Rafael *et al.* (1997) Trust in large organizations. *American Economic Review, Papers and Proceedings*, 87 (2), 333–338.

Laffont, Jean-Jaques and Rochet, Jean-Charles (1997) Collusion in organizations. *Scandinavian Journal of Economics*, 99 (4), 485–495.

Laffont, Jean-Jaques and Tirole, Jean (1993) *A Theory of Incentives in Procurement and Regulation.* Cambridge: The MIT Press.

Luhmann, Niklas (1969/1993) *Legitimation durch Verfahren.* Frankfurt am Main: Suhrkamp.

Mackaay, Ejan (1998) Emergence of legal rules. In: Newman, P. (Ed): *The New Palgrave Dictionary of Economics and the Law.* pp. 29–34 London: Macmillan Reference Limited.

Malinowski, Bonislaw (1926) *Crime and Custom in Savage Society.* London: Routledge and Kegan Paul.

Marris, P. and Somerset, A. (1971) *African Businessmen.* London: Routledge and Kegan Paul.

Mookherjee, Dilip and Png, I. P. L. (1995) Corruptible law enforcers: how should they be compensated? *The Economic Journal,* 105, 145–159.

Moore, Sally Falk (1986) *Social Facts and Fabricants: Customary Law in Kilimanjaro 1880–1980.* New York: Cambridge University Press.

Naím, Moisés (1995) *Latin America's Journey to the Market. From Macroeconomic Shocks to Institutional Therapy.* San Francisco: ICS Press.

North, Douglass C. (1981) *Structure and Change in Economic History.* New York: W.W. Norton Company, Inc.

   (1990) *Institutions, Institutional Change, and Economic Performance.* Cambridge: Cambridge University Press.

Olson, M. (1982) *The Rise and Decline of Nations.* New Haven: Yale University Press.

Ostrom, E. (1986) An agenda for the study of institutions. *Public Choice,* 48, 3–25.

   (1990) *Governing the Commons: The Evolution of Institutions for Collective Action.* Cambridge: Cambridge University Press.

Pejovich, Svetozar (1997): Law, Tradition, and the Transition in Eastern Europe. *The Independent Review,* II (2), 243–254.

Pinckney, Thomas C. and Kimuyu, Peter K. (1994): Land tenure reform in East Africa: good, bad or unimportant. *Journal of African Economies,* 3, 1–28.

Platteau, Jean-Philippe (1996) *Traditional Sharing Norms as an Obstacle to Economic Growth in Tribal Societies.* Faculté des Sciences économiques et sociales, Centre de Recherche en Economie du Développement. Namur: Facultes Universitaires Notre-Dame de la Paix.

Popisil, L. (1958) *Kapauka Papuans and their Law.* New Haven, CT: Yale University Press.

Posner, E. (1996a) The regulation of groups: the influence of legal and non-legal sanctions on collective action. *University of Chicago Law Review,* 63 (133), 133–197.

   (1996b) Law, economics, and inefficient norms. *University of Pennsylvania Law Review,* 144, 1697–1744.

Posner, Richard A. (1980) A theory of primitive society with special reference to Law. *Journal of Law and Economics,* XXIII (1), 1–53.

   (1992) *Economic Analysis of Law.* Boston, Toronto, London: Little, Brown and Company.

Putnam, Robert (1993) *Making Democracy Work: Civic Traditions in Modern Italy.* Princeton, NJ: Princeton University Press.

Reynolds, Lloyd G. (1985) *Economic Growth in the Third World, 1850–1980.* New Haven: Yale University Press.

Romer, David (1984) The theory of social custom: a modification and some extensions. *Quarterly Journal of Economics*, XCIX (4), 717–727.

Röpke, Wilhelm (1950) *The Social Crisis of Our Time*. Chicago: The University of Chicago Press.

Rose-Ackerman, Susan (1985) Inalienability and the theory of property rights. *Columbia Law Review*, 85 (5), 931–969.

Temple, Jonathan and Johnson, Paul A. (1998) Social capability and economic growth. *Quarterly Journal of Economics*, 113, 965–990.

Thalheim, K.C. (1955) Zum Problem der Einheitlichkeit der Wirtschaftspolitik. pp. 577–587. In: Muhs K. (ed.): *Festgabe für Georg Jahn*. Berlin.

Thomas, John W. and Grindle, Merilee S. (1990) After the decision: implementing policy reforms in developing countries. *World Development*, 18 (8), 1163–1181.

Tirole, Jean (1986) Hierarchies and bureaucracies: on the role of collusion in organizations. *The Journal of Law, Economics & Organization*, 2 (2), 181–214.

   (1992) Collusion and the theory of organizations. pp. 151–206. In: Laffont, J.-J. (ed): *Advances in Economic Theory*. Cambridge: Cambridge University Press.

Tuchtfeldt, Egon (1960) Zur Frage der Systemkonformität wirtschaftspolitischer Maßnahmen. pp. 203–238. In. H.-J. Seraphim (ed.) *Zur Grundlegung wirtschaftspolitischer Konzeptionen*. Berlin: Duncker and Humblot.

Tyler, Tom R. (1990) *Why People Obey the Law*. New Haven: Yale University Press.

Ullman-Margalit, Edna (1978) *The Emergence of Norms*. Oxford: Oxford University Press.

Voigt, Stefan and Kiwit, Daniel (1998) The role and evolution of beliefs, habits, moral norms, and institutions. pp. 83–108 in: Harbert Giersch (ed.) *The Merits and Limits of Markets*. Berlin: Springer.

Weber, Max (1905/1993) *The Protestant Ethic and the Spirit of Capitalism*. London: Routledge.

Wegner, Gerhard (1997) Economic policy from an evolutionary perspective: a new approach. *Journal of Institutional and Theoretical Economics (JITE)*, 153 (3), 485–509.

Wilson, James Q. (1989) *Bureaucracy: What Government Agencies Do and Why They Do It*. New York: Basic Books.

Witt, Ulrich (1989) The evolution of economic institutions as a propagating process. *Public Choice*, 62, 155–172.

   (1999) Multiple equilibria, critical masses, and institutional change: the coup d' état problem. pp.286–299. In: Bowles, S. *et al.* (eds.) *The Politics and Economics of Power*. London, New York: Routledge.

5

The role of evaluation in foreign aid programmes

Bertin Martens

1. INTRODUCTION

Chapter 2 examined the impact on aid performance of information asymmetries between principals and agents within an official aid agency. This chapter analyses the impact of information asymmetries between the aid agency, donors and taxpayers and aid services suppliers. Later on in the chapter, information asymmetries between the agency and its political principals will also be added. The main purpose of this chapter is to demonstrate how these information asymmetries explain some of the observed behavioural characteristics of aid organisations and how foreign aid performance is to a large extent determined by donor country domestic policy concerns, not only by policies in the recipient country.

A major cause of these fundamental information asymmetries is inherent to foreign aid: in contrast to domestic transfer programmes, foreign aid programmes transfer wealth to intended beneficiaries outside the constituency of the taxpayers who pay for it and the politicians who decide on it. Foreign beneficiaries have no direct political leverage on donor country decision-makers. It is somewhat hard to see why donor country politicians would use voters' taxes to satisfy the needs and wishes of non-voters, unless voters have a stake in it too – that is, unless there is domestic demand for foreign aid transfers.

The geographical and political dislocation between donors and beneficiaries results in a broken information feedback loop that induces performance bias in aid programmes because it has an asymmetric impact. It effectively neutralises the influence of the final beneficiaries in the recipient country on political decision-making in the donor country. This leaves only three players in the decision-making arena: aid services suppliers, donors and taxpayers. Aid services suppliers have easier access to information at a lower opportunity cost than donors and taxpayers. Services suppliers have first-hand information because of their day-to-day involvement in project implementation and their presence and activities in the recipient country. Taxpayers depend on second-hand information provided by intermediaries; it would be far too costly for them to obtain first-hand information. The relative cost of information thus favours aid services suppliers and makes it easier for them to further their interests at the expense of taxpayers.

The broken feedback loop and information cost disadvantage of taxpayers can only be restored by an explicit new information mechanism, which we label generically as 'evaluation'. An explicit evaluation function is inherent to the nature of foreign aid programmes, much more so than domestic transfer programmes where other low-cost performance feedback channels exist, including direct information from beneficiaries.

However, because of the peculiar incentives and institutional structure of foreign aid programmes, evaluation feedback mechanisms are not independent from, but subject to, political forces. We will demonstrate that evaluation plays a key role in establishing a political performance equilibrium for foreign aid programmes, though that equilibrium is not necessarily efficient in terms of satisfying taxpayers' objectives of genuine wealth transfers. Evaluation serves to maintain this political equilibrium and is, in itself, unable to enhance aid performance. Manipulation of the quality of evaluation reports helps politicians to drive an informational wedge between the objectives of taxpayers and aid services suppliers, thereby maximising their votes but reducing satisfaction for both interest groups.[1] This efficiency loss is the opportunity cost to be paid for political entrepreneurship that allows these programmes to exist in the first place.

The structure of this chapter is as follows. In Section 2 I examine how public administrations operate, in general, and how

---

[1] Votes should not be interpreted narrowly as the number of votes during an election. In this paper, it is interpreted broadly as general support for the politician.

inefficiencies can occur because obfuscation of performance information is facilitated by the nature of their work as well as by political incentives. In Section 3 I compare this with the incentives faced by foreign aid agencies, a special sub-set of public administrations, and demonstrate that obfuscation of information is expected to be worse because of the incentives structure generated by the structure of demand for foreign aid. I develop a principal–agent model to explain the behaviour of different types of agents in foreign aid processes – politicians, suppliers and aid agencies – and relate the findings from the model to some of the empirically observed characteristics of the behaviour of foreign aid agencies. Evaluation of suppliers' performance is necessary to avoid moral hazard. But the quantity and quality of evaluation reporting is determined by political objectives. The remaining sections develop special applications of the standard model, such as variations in the quality of evaluations, and introduce moral hazard between politicians and their aid agencies.

2. PUBLIC ADMINISTRATIONS AND THE EVALUATION OF TRANSFERS

Anthony Downs (1967) already observed that, contrary to private profit-seeking companies, public administrations usually have multiple and hard-to-define objectives that are not easily quantifiable or even verifiable. The absence of a clearly defined trade-off between these objectives leaves room for discretion in the allocation of resources. Public administrations are not owned by shareholders with a single common objective – profit – but by politicians who rarely share objectives, have different priorities and thereby create incoherent trade-offs. Consequently, it is very difficult to establish an efficiency measure of the activities of public administrations and their 'owners', the politicians. It is difficult and costly to measure their actual performance and often impossible to define a single objectively verifiable – let alone quantifiable – indicator for that purpose. Down's insights have been formalised recently in the principal–agent literature (Holmstrom and Milgrom, 1991; Aghion and Tirole, 1997; Tirole, 1994). That literature is based on information asymmetry between a principal and the agent(s) to whom tasks are delegated. As the principal has imperfect information on the activities of agent(s), the risks of moral hazard and adverse selection are real. Well-designed incentives may reduce this risk. As delegation is a common practice in public administrations, the findings of the principal–agent literature are easily applicable.

Despite the lessons from the principal–agent literature, the neo-classical branch of public choice theory maintains that public administrations and their owners, the politicians, nevertheless behave rather efficiently, at least in a democratic system where voters can vote politicians in and out of office (Wittman, 1995). Competition between politicians, combined with voters' information on government programmes, will lead to voters choosing those politicians that maximise voters' wealth (Becker, 1983). Voters are the final consumers and thus the ultimate evaluators of their (in)efficiency. Even though programme results may not be easily verifiable or measurable, voters' sentiment is assumed to be a good programme performance indicator.

In a recent paper, Johnson and Libecap (1999) question the efficiency hypothesis. The Achilles heel of the hypothesis is the assumption that voters are well-informed about government programmes. Johnson and Libecap argue that, under competitive political systems, politicians have an incentive to inform the direct beneficiaries of government transfer programmes but, at the same time, obfuscate information about the actual costs and benefits of the programme for tax-paying voters who are not direct beneficiaries. They illustrate this with the case of the ethanol subsidy programme in the USA, whereby voters are being persuaded in favour of a subsidy for corn-based additives into petrol through presumed environmental, rural development and energy security benefits. Politicians have an incentive to obfuscate information for non-direct beneficiaries. This is made easy because of the technical and economic complexity of the programme. Considerable expertise and time is required to find out about the true nature of the costs and benefits. The direct beneficiaries, in this case corn farmers who receive better prices for their corn, are of course kept well-informed about the transfers they receive and the benefits they derive from it. They conclude that competitive political markets are not efficient because there is an incentive to distort information. Public administrations have no incentive to upset the information equilibrium with reports. Doing so would probably eject administrators from office, or at least result in reprisal actions. A critical evaluation study of the US ethanol programme was sharply attacked and the authors' careers suffered severely.

Johnson and Libecap's findings can also be applied to foreign aid programmes, taking into account the particular informational features that distinguish foreign from domestic transfer programmes.

3. FOREIGN AID TRANSFERS AND AID AGENCIES

Foreign aid programmes are run by aid agencies, a sub-set of public administrations, and have a very specific characteristic: the intended beneficiaries of the fiscal transfers live outside the country of the taxpayers and their elected politicians. This immediately begs the question 'Where does the domestic demand for foreign aid come from: why would people express a demand for something of which they are not beneficiaries?' There is also no doubt that the neo-classical competitive efficiency hypothesis of public administration cannot be applicable here. The intended beneficiaries are not voters in the country that pays for the aid and thus have no real leverage over the politicians who approve these programmes. Why then would vote-maximising politicians transfer wealth to these intended beneficiaries? Where does the real demand for foreign aid programmes come from?

We first examine potential domestic sources of demand for foreign aid, including the objectives of each of these sources. From that, we derive an incentive structure for the performance of various actors involved in foreign aid.

The demand for foreign aid

Politicians who vote on foreign aid programmes may have various constituencies (with voting power) and their interests in mind:

(a) Taxpayers: a genuine desire to redistribute income to the poor, solidarity, cognitive dissonance when being confronted with pictures of the poor and needy, etc. are all reasons for the existence of a real demand for foreign aid by taxpayers;

(b) Suppliers of aid goods and services: these are commercial companies, individual consultants and sometimes academic institutions who earn (part of) their livelihood in the provision of goods and services required to run aid programmes. Foreign aid is 'business as usual' for them. It boosts their export markets and may sometimes be used as an (implicit) subsidy for their commercial export operations.

(c) Non-governmental aid agencies and lobby groups: they are in a more ambiguous position. On the one hand, they constitute an organised way to represent the taxpayers' genuine demand for redistribution of wealth to the poor. On the other hand, many of these organisations live from official aid funds that are being channelled through them. They take on the characteristics of bureaucracies, including competition among agents for jobs, status and careers inside the organisation and of course moral hazard in internal principal–agent relationships.

(d) Administrators in foreign aid agencies: these can be counted as a group that has an interest in promoting foreign aid programmes: it provides them with jobs and careers. However, while private agents are driven by fairly easily verifiable profit indicators, performance indicators for public agents are not easily verifiable, so that their performance is much more subject to distortion. Also, the distinction between private service suppliers and public administrators may not be very clear. There is usually a steady flow of agents between both categories, and the statutes of some agents in public aid agencies may take characteristics of private aid suppliers (fixed-term contracts with no career prospects or security of employment, for instance).

The specific incentives of administrators in aid agencies, and their potential impact on aid performance, have already been discussed in Chapter 2; the present chapter will not discuss that subject. We will also leave aside, for the time being, the incentives of non-governmental aid agencies and lobby groups. As they combine the characteristics of service suppliers and taxpayers, they will be brought back into the picture after we have analysed the impact of governmental aid agencies' 'pure' strategy players.

Aid services suppliers are the direct domestic beneficiaries of aid programmes in a politician's constituency: they get the direct financial benefits from the fiscal transfer programme. In return, they pay the opportunity cost of the effort to implement the programmes. As profit maximisers, they aim to maximise the difference between the direct benefit and the opportunity cost of the effort. The indirect domestic benefits accrue to the taxpayers: their genuine demand for income redistribution and 'development' is supposedly satisfied through the implementation of transfer programmes by the aid agency. In return, they pay taxes for that satisfaction. They will aim to maximise their consumer surplus, net of taxes. Vote-maximising politicians will try to satisfy the – often opposing – interests of these two constituencies. How they can do so, is explored in the next sections. Note that, in this model, the existence of a demand for aid by the intended beneficiaries in the recipient countries is not a necessary condition for the emergence of foreign aid programmes.

Politicians

Assume that a donor country has a fixed total tax revenue (T), to be allocated to a finite number of public spending programmes, T_i, such that $\Sigma T_i \leq T$. One of these spending programmes is foreign aid, $T_a \in \forall T_i$. Politicians in that country will compete for votes by making promises to their constituency and, in the case of re-election, show that they can actually deliver on these promises with respect to both financial allocations T_i and performance targets B_i for each of these programmes. Politicians will profile themselves on T_i and B_i in such a way that it maximises their expected votes.

Taxpayers vote for those politicians who seem to be most promising in terms of maximising their perceived consumer surplus $(B_i - T_i)$ with respect to their preferred programmes. Implementation of programmes is delegated to commercial services suppliers. Services suppliers vote for politicians who maximise their profits $\Pi_i = (T_i - C_i)$: the contractually agreed reward T_i minus the opportunity cost C_i of the effort to implement programme i. The number of suppliers is usually very small compared to the number of beneficiaries and one would therefore expect votes from suppliers to be marginal if not irrelevant in the electoral process. However, we assume that suppliers can donate part of their profits to the campaign funds of politicians, which enables them to generate more votes. For this reason, the number of votes raised by suppliers' support is not marginal.

For domestic spending programmes, we assume that voters have the means to observe directly whether politicians live up to their promises on T_i and B_i: they live in the recipient constituency and are often direct beneficiaries of the programmes. In the case of foreign aid spending programmes however, voters depend on information (I) provided by the implementing agency, lobby groups and commercial suppliers to these programmes. Suppliers, on the contrary, are assumed to be perfectly well-informed about their own financial benefits from the programme as well as about real programme performance (since they implement the programmes); they do not require any additional information.

Votes for politicians are determined by profits for suppliers and perceived consumer surplus for citizens. Politicians aim to maximise the following function:

$$\max V = \Sigma_i f((T_i - C_i); I(B_i - T_i))$$
$$\text{s.t.} \quad \Sigma_i T_i \leq T \tag{5.1}$$

Politicians have two instrumental variables at their disposal to maximise votes: the allocation of taxes across various public spending programmes T_i, including foreign aid T_a, and the information (I) given to taxpayers/voters on both allocations T_i and performance B_i.

In practice, the politician's leverage on setting T_i is weak. The allocation of T_i is determined by voters' preferences – which are exogenous in this model – and the segment in the voters' market that the politician intends to occupy (left, right, pro-aid, etc.). Implementation of T_i is then delegated to a government agency that is in charge of ensuring programme performance B. Performance of aid programmes is not an instrumental variable for politicians. It depends on suppliers and on incentives that government agencies give them by using part of the foreign aid budget to carry out performance audits, monitoring and evaluation, during and after implementation.[2] Consequently, performance is only indirectly influenced by politicians, through decisions on evaluation.

This leaves information for voters as the only instrumental variable for politicians. As explained above, politicians' room for manoeuvre with information on domestic transfer programmes is usually very limited since many voters are direct beneficiaries and have first-hand information. In the case of foreign aid however, no such direct feedback loop exists. Voters depend on information provided by the aid agency, non-governmental organisations (NGOs) or other media. This gives a key political role to evaluation studies by aid agencies. Because of their hold on the aid agency and the evaluations that it carries out, politicians have privileged access to information on programme performance, and the use of that information. However, politicians do not have a monopoly on information, at least not in democratic countries where there is competition with other sources of information. We will show that the amount and quality of information that aid agencies gather on programme performance is the politicians' most important instrumental variable. In the next sections, we examine how politicians can use that variable to influence the behaviour of foreign aid services suppliers and aid implementing agencies in order to maximise votes, and how that influences aid programme performance. This effectively endogenises foreign aid performance as a function of domestic policy considerations.

The suppliers

Politicians delegate implementation of foreign aid programmes to a foreign aid agency which, in turn, delegates the tasks to be performed in the beneficiary countries to private subcontractors or aid services suppliers. This is a standard implementation arrangement, applied by most bilateral and multilateral aid agencies. The total aid budget, T_a, is allocated among various projects that are usually contracted out through competitive tender procedures. The

---

[2] In this paper, all types and sources of information on programme performance are brought together under the generic label 'evaluation'. No distinction is made between audit, monitoring and evaluation.

winner of each tendered project receives an agreed amount t_i (with $\Sigma t_i \leq T_a$) upon successful achievement of the project objectives B^*_i, as described in the terms of reference.

Supplier performance B requires effort with an opportunity cost C:

$$B = f(C) \quad \text{with } f' > 0 \text{ and } f'' < 0 \tag{5.2}$$

The agreed performance target B^* is reached at an opportunity cost C^*. The suppliers are free to choose their effort level and thus the degree of achievement of the objective B. We assume that the suppliers know their true effort and performance, at no additional cost and independently of any evaluation efforts by the aid agency or other interested parties. The aid agencies, by contrast, have to invest a real cost E in evaluation (to be deducted from T_a) in order to obtain information on suppliers' performance. Because of this information opportunity cost, there is potential for moral hazard and adverse selection in the contract between aid agencies and the aid services suppliers. The suppliers' effort will depend on the aid agencies' ability to monitor their actual performance. If their performance is found out to be significantly below B^*, they will not be paid at all for their efforts $(t_i = 0)$.

Information on supplier performance can come from two sources: the aid agency itself can produce evaluation reports, or external observers such as aid lobby groups, NGOs and the press can reveal information on the project's true performance. Each source of information presents a risk for the supplier of being found out and not being paid his contractually agreed reward t_i. The risk of being found out by the agency (p) depends on the resources that the agency allocates to evaluation (E) and the discrepancy between *ex-post* observed and *ex-ante* agreed performance $(B^* - B)$: the wider the discrepancy, the higher the risk that it will be noticed. The amount spent on evaluation (E) by the agency and the risk of being found out by an outside source of information (p_x) are exogenous constants for the supplier. Total risk p for the supplier can be defined as:

$$p = g((B^* - B), E, p_x) \quad \text{with } 0 \leq p \leq 1 \tag{5.3}$$

The supplier's expected profit (Π) or loss on the aid operation thus amounts to:

$$\Pi = (1 - p)t_i - C_i \qquad (5.4)$$

Effort, or opportunity cost C, is the supplier's only instrumental variable. His optimal effort level will be reached when his expected profit is maximised. Assuming that p_x is exogenously given, the supplier's project effort C will be determined by the agency's evaluation effort E.

As t_i is fixed, it would be irrational for any supplier to invest beyond C^* and only a fully risk-aversive supplier would invest as much as C^* to achieve B^*. A supplier with normal risk aversion will be underperforming as long as $p < 1$. The actual level of C and B depends on the shape and properties of the production function in equation (5.2) and the risk function in equation (5.3).

The supplier's actual effort and the resulting project performance depend on evaluation incentives provided by the aid agency. Agency investments in evaluation will improve contractor performance but not up to the planned performance target B^*, unless E is such that $p = 1$, which is unlikely in a world with hard-to-measure objectives. Suppliers will anticipate agency evaluation efforts and revise their own optimal effort level upwards to take into account the increased risk of detection. On the other hand, an upward revision of efforts will narrow the gap between actual and planned B, and thereby decrease again the risk of detection. Reputation effects can of course play a role here. If the supplier's next contract depends on his performance in the previous contract, he may increase his efforts because the stakes are higher. Still, it will be below C^* because the risk of being found out lowers with smaller divergence between B and B^*.

A digression into consultants' markets

The above-described model of aid services suppliers behaviour is worth a short digression into empirical applications. The strong link between suppliers' effort and agencies' evaluation efforts has important implications for foreign aid tender procedures and tender markets. Fully risk-aversive suppliers are unlikely to win tenders since their best price is higher than that offered by less risk-aversive competitors. Willingness to take risks will have a major influence on tender results. Following Gresham's law, 'bad suppliers will drive out good suppliers'. On average, suppliers who take more risks and make less effort to achieve project objectives, stand a higher risk of being found out. But that risk becomes verifiable *ex-post* of contract signature only and often *ex-post* of project implementation, when it is too late and/or very costly to correct implementation problems. There are basically two ways to reduce these post-contractual risks: invest more in *ex-ante* information on the quality of the bidders or make it exceedingly costly for them to take implementation risks. Both require performance evaluation.

Ex-ante information requires a track record, an evaluation of previous projects implemented by the bidders. This turns single-project tenders into a repeated game between the suppliers and the agency, whereby reputation and credibility play a role. The absence of mechanisms to check suppliers' performance under previous contracts and use performance track records in tender procedures, invites opportunism and facilitates the life of 'body-shops' and free-riders in the suppliers' community, driving more credible (but more costly, because they make more efforts) suppliers out of the market. Agencies that do not use formal or informal performance track records tend to end up at the lower end of the suppliers' quality spectrum: they get the cheapest suppliers with low risk-aversion. The trend to switch from traditional investment projects to policy and institutional reforms, makes detailed specification and verification of project outputs more difficult and increases the probability of moral hazard and adverse selection in aid services supplies.

So far, we assumed that evaluations are handled in-house by the aid agency. But evaluations may also be contracted out to private for-profit aid services suppliers, just like any other aid project, of course taking care that no direct conflict of interest occurs in order not to affect the report's credibility. While most evaluation work in the World Bank is done by its own officials, the European Commission (EC) contracts out virtually all evaluations to for-profit companies.

In-house evaluations are not credible unless they are done by an independent group of employees.[3] Full separation between the aid agency and the evaluation function is not necessarily a good solution, however. It may avoid some of the agency problems and misalignment of incentives but can not overcome the information problem inherent in fiscal transfer programmes. Courts of Auditors are a good example. Their reports are not constrained by internal agency problems or political constraints. However, they usually get caught in heavy political crossfire between interest groups, aimed at discrediting the report. As they anticipate this counter-information attack, they have a tendency to 'sharpen' the messages in their reports, which only intensifies the information competition but contributes little to clarifying the picture for taxpayers.

Aid agencies contracting out evaluations to so-called 'independent' for-profit experts is often seen as a means to enhance the credibility of evaluation reports without running into the problems of fully independent evaluations. However, there may be biased incentives here too. Reputation effects and peer group pressure will ensure that these 'independent consultants' temper their critical remarks. Consultants who do evaluation studies have no incentive to reveal precise and controversial information. It makes their report vulnerable to heavy criticism and long-drawn discussions without any increase in their remuneration. The consultants–evaluators are no stakeholders in the outcome of the evaluation. On the contrary, consultants are commercial aid services suppliers and have their own commercial interests. Evaluation studies usually represent just a small share of their market. Their own market may be at stake when they produce critical reports. Commercial evaluation consultants may need to be 'protected' when working on evaluation studies, to avoid retaliation from competitors and even from the aid agency itself.

Consultants often produce imprecisely formulated 'woolly' reports. This may be due to several misaligned incentives. Firstly, once their study contract is signed (and revenue is fixed), they have an incentive to minimise information gathering costs, subject to a credibility constraint. This induces strong moral hazard, especially

---

[3] The Operations Evaluation Department benefits from some degree of independence of the rest of the Bank though. The Director General reports directly to the Board and is explicitly excluded from career prospects in the Bank. His collaborators are not however.

so because evaluation administrators are not in a position to verify coverage and accuracy of the consultants' data set. Secondly, consultants whose main market is in foreign aid contracts, adapt to the incentives in that market. They will show a tendency towards inputs-bias (see Chapter 2) and will not seek to reveal results that could have an unsettling effect on that market.

This does not necessarily imply that consultants consciously seek to deceive or misreport their findings; rather, they act in accordance with the incentives provided by their environment. Market pressure is usually exerted in a much more subtle and implicit way. Consultants will stick to a particular vocabulary and jargon that is imprecisely defined and leaves margins for interpretation. 'Woolly' language is not only the trademark of the bureaucrat to protect himself against the uncertainties of a multiple principals and objectives environment; it is also adopted by his agents outside the bureaucracy for the same reasons.

Consultants who work almost exclusively for aid agencies often become themselves generalists, like administrators in aid agencies. Their comparative advantage resides in their ability to understand the (political) logic of the aid administration and to produce reports that are relevant to solving the political problems that the administration is confronted with – which are unlikely to be identical to the problems of the intended beneficiaries. This phenomenon of institutional 'isomorphism' between a large organisation and a smaller that is heavily dependent on it, is not new and has been frequently observed in a variety of organisational settings (DiMaggio and Powell, 1993).

The aid agency

For the time being, we will assume that there is no moral hazard between politicians who exercise political oversight of the activities of the aid agency (a minister or secretary of state for development co-operation) and the agency administrators to which they delegate the task of implementing aid programmes; their interests are assumed to be identical. Later on, we will relax this assumption when we consider multiple political principals. A key question for politicians and their aid agencies is to know how much of the total aid budget (T_a) they should invest in evaluation (E). That depends on the politician's dependence on the two main domestic lobby groups for aid, taxpayers and aid services suppliers.

Consider the extreme case of full collusion of interest between suppliers and the aid agency or politician. The agency would not invest in evaluation at all so as to make life easier for its suppliers. Consequently, $E = 0$ and suppliers' efforts to achieve performance targets B^* will be at their lowest level. The agency's mission is reduced to maximising suppliers' profit. Still, suppliers' efforts $C > 0$ because other sources of information, such as press and NGOs remain a real risk ($p_x > 0$) of discovery of suppliers' underperformance ($B < B^*$). If any of these sources publish an account of serious underperformance in an aid project run by the agency, this could reflect badly on the agency's and suppliers' reputation and credibility. It might negatively affect the overall budget allocated to aid and thus the overall power of the aid agency. Note that the risk of an external source discovering such a problem increases when $E \rightarrow 0$: suppliers will anticipate the absence of evaluation by the agency and reduce their efforts, so that the discrepancy between B^* and B will increase, thereby increasing the likelihood of discovery of the discrepancy. Suppliers will invest a minimum level of effort to counter any perceived risks of discovery by external information sources.

Consider the other extreme case with a politician and agency directly answerable to voters only. Its sole mission would be to maximise consumer surplus for taxpayers, that is maximise $B - T$ which, in the case of a fixed aid budget T_a, boils down to maximising performance B. In that case, the agency's only instrumental variable is the share of that aid budget to be set aside for evaluation purposes. The agency's behaviour would be to maximise B, subject to the budget constraint T_a.[4] Assume that B is cardinal and all possible projects $1 \rightarrow n$ that can be financed from T_a are ranked in descending order of B.[5]

$$\max B = \max \Sigma_1^n B_i(t_i, E) \qquad (5.5)$$
$$\text{s.t.} \quad \Sigma t_i + E \leq T_a$$

[4] This study does not investigate the question how an agency chooses its projects. It assumes that the agency has a ranking order of preferred projects and has to decide on the marginal project to be implemented, against the marginal evaluation effort.

[5] Cardinality of B implies that aid has a single and quantifiable objective. This is obviously a gross oversimplification of reality, to be adjusted below.

If the entire aid budget were spent on projects and nothing on evaluation, moral hazard would be maximised and erode aid performance to a minimum. The choice for an optimal allocation between E and Σt_i is determined by suppliers' risk aversion, $\partial p / \partial E$. The equilibrium allocation E^* will be reached when the marginal increase in B of an additional unit of T_a spent on evaluation, is equal to the marginal increase in B of an additional unit spent on the next project in the ranking: $\partial B / \partial E = \partial B / \partial t_{n+1}$. E^* is the amount allocated by an independent agency to evaluation activities; it ensures that voters get maximum value for their tax money.

However, in real worlds, politicians are put in power by political majorities that represent multiple interests, including taxpayers claiming a genuine aid effort and suppliers claiming support for their business interests. Politicians, in turn, delegate the task of implementing foreign aid programmes to an aid agency. The aid agency works in the interest of its political supervisor and political constraints influence the optimal amount of evaluation E^*. The mission of the aid agency in that case is neither to maximise suppliers' profit Π nor voters' consumer surplus $(B - T)$ nor programme performance B; it's mission is to help politicians maximise votes V. How does this affect the allocation of T between evaluation and projects and thus the actual performance of foreign aid programmes?

The politician in charge of supervising the aid agency will have to combine the interests of suppliers and taxpayers. He will have to perform a careful balancing act, somewhere in between $E = E^*$ – where voter's interests are maximised – and $E = 0$ that maximises suppliers' profit. The political equilibrium value for E, E°, will necessarily be lower than E^*. E° depends on the weights of suppliers and taxpayers in the politicians' vote functions. Politicians whose constituency is biased towards taxpayers who favour foreign aid programmes will tend to de-emphasise suppliers' interests; the contrary is true for politicians who are heavily dependent on campaign support from suppliers' lobbies.

Consequently, foreign aid performance will be lower in this political equilibrium situation: $B(E^\circ) < B(E^*)$. This illustrates once more the main point in this chapter and in this entire book: aid performance is determined by domestic policy concerns in the donor country, not only by policies in the recipient country. One would also be tempted to conclude that the introduction of politicians in this model constitutes a dead-weight loss for taxpayers. We will mitigate that tentative conclusion in the next sections.

Note that in this model, there is no need for the agency to actually publish evaluation reports. Evaluation reports are not meant to increase transparency and accountability towards the public and are used for internal management, early warning and defensive purposes only. Many aid agencies are in this situation. They keep monitoring, audit and evaluation reports as internal documents. The motivation to do so can only be political, since the aid agency and politicians have no incentive to ensure better aid performance, on the contrary. That incentive can only come from taxpayers/voters who, in the absence of information on programme performance, are of course unable to use their leverage on politicians.

4. THE QUALITY OF EVALUATIONS

So far, we assumed that the government budget allocated to foreign aid (T_a) is determined by voters' preferences and that actual aid programme performance (B) is determined by the incentives given to suppliers, through evaluation of their performance. The share of the total aid budget that is allocated to evaluation (E) is the key instrumental variable for politicians and their aid agencies. The preceding section explained how that variable can be used to maximise votes for political principals. However, that analysis was based on the implicit assumption that there is a one-to-one link between votes (V) and foreign aid performance (B). In reality, that link is not constant and depends on variations in the quality of the information available to citizens on programme performance.

Information can be manipulated for strategic (political) purposes. Contrary to domestic aid programmes, where taxpayers can experience the performance of programmes themselves and obtain first-hand information, in foreign aid programmes taxpayers pay for the programme but do not get the benefits. Evaluation reports therefore play an important role in the information feedback loop on foreign aid. Taxpayers need information provided by all kinds of evaluation reports to find out about the true benefits delivered by their aid. This provides politicians, and their aid agencies, with an opportunity to use evaluations, not only to influence suppliers' performance but also to influence voters/taxpayers' attitudes towards foreign aid programmes. The quality of information about foreign aid programmes, as revealed through evaluations, is the subject of the present section.

The quality, or accuracy, of an evaluation can be defined as the probability that the target value of a programme performance parameter, B^*, falls within a certain confidence interval around its mean value observed during the evaluation. We assume that the standard deviation on the observed value of B is negatively correlated with the relative cost of the evaluation: the more money (E_i) is spent on an evaluation, relative to the size or budget of the aid programme (t_i) to be evaluated, the lower the standard deviation (σ) around the observed mean and the higher the degree of accuracy of the report:

$$\sigma(B) = f(t_i/E_i) \tag{5.6}$$

The quality of evaluations may also be affected by the ease and cost of measurement of crucial project performance variables. For instance, traditional investment projects, such as roads, schools and hospitals, generate relatively easily observable performance targets. By contrast, institutional reform projects, including policy reform, generate less tangible outputs, the quality of which is more difficult to observe. As such, the shift in contemporary aid programmes from investment to institutional reforms has made evaluation more costly and less accurate.

Wider standard deviations – less accurate reports – present a number of advantages for politicians and aid agencies. Firstly, the wider the standard deviation, the easier it is to claim that the observed performance B falls within a given confidence interval around the target value B^*. This comforts taxpayers/voters that the targets have been achieved and keeps up their willingness to pay for these fiscal transfers.

Secondly, the corollary of this statement is that, with wider standard deviations, it is more difficult to prove that a project has effectively missed its target B^*. This gives programme critics a harder time. Countervailing information offensives by lobby groups, NGOs or press may have a hard time to prove that B^* was not reached. Hard-to-measure programme performance facilitates obfuscation of information for the taxpayer.

Thirdly, it leaves suppliers reasonably at peace. If they can anticipate 'woolly' reporting, with wide standard deviations, they can safely lower their efforts and allow B to deviate further from B^*, thereby increasing their profits. As such, variations in the quality of evaluation reports help politicians to drive a wedge between the opposing interests of suppliers and voters and soften the stand-off between their objectives. Suppliers can lower their efforts and increase profits, while voters remain satisfied. For the same allocation of E and T, the number of votes rises. It helps politicians to earn more votes from both groups.

However, there are also limits to the freedom of politicians and aid agencies to influence the quality of evaluation reports, both positively and negatively. To prove this, let's consider two extreme cases of collusion of interest, firstly between the politician and aid lobby groups, and secondly between the politician and aid service suppliers.

In the first case, the politician derives most of his votes from pro-aid lobby groups such as NGOs. He decides to play it hard on aid suppliers, to increase funds for evaluation and to increase the relative cost of evaluations so as to improve accuracy. The suppliers reluctantly increase their efforts but also counterattack by producing their own 'contra-evaluation' reports, thereby blurring the picture for taxpayers. 'Contra' reports are not designed to prove or reject the hypothesis that the target has been achieved ; rather, they intend to undermine the credibility of the agency's evaluation report by focusing on particular aspects that may easily be put in doubt. As a result, voters are confused, aid performance is not improved because funds are diverted to counter-reports rather than increased efforts, and the politician loses credibility: all parties lose in this scenario.

In the second case, the politician is voted into power with the help of commercial aid service suppliers. Collusion of interest between politician and suppliers is likely to occur. The politician instructs the aid agency to reduce investments in evaluation and, consequently, to reduce the accuracy of reports on programme performance. Voters might still be pleased with woolly reports, but the woollier they are the easier it becomes for aid lobby groups, NGOs and press to cast doubt over their accuracy and produce counter-reports. Again, this confuses voters and will affect the politician's and aid agency's credibility, thereby reducing votes. Clearly, the risk that outsiders cast doubt over reports is a limiting factor on the agency's margin for manoeuvre with the accuracy of evaluation reports. A minimum degree of credibility has to be kept.

It now looks as if we have equipped the politician with two instruments to win votes, for a given aid budget T_a: the amount allocated to evaluation and the quality of evaluation studies. The first instruments can be used to trade off the conflicting interests of taxpayers (genuine wealth redistribution) and aid services suppliers (profit). The second allows politicians to drive an informational wedge between these interests, to the disadvantage of taxpayers' interests and the advantage of politicians and suppliers. In fact, these are not two independent instrumental variables. Once the share of evaluation E in the total foreign aid budget T_a has been decided, the average overall cost of evaluations $E / \Sigma t_i$ has also been fixed. What remains undecided is the distribution of the evaluation budget across the various aid projects t_i. How are politicians going to use this remaining degree of freedom?

The obvious solution would be to allocate relatively larger evaluation budgets and produce relatively more accurate evaluation reports on projects that are reasonably well-run and/or politically less contentious. Political constituency considerations may however change that allocation. A politician whose constituency is mainly based in NGO circles favouring genuine aid efforts may decide to reverse that allocation; politicians whose constituency is mainly based in suppliers' circles, may further bias the allocation towards potentially less contentious projects.

5. MULTIPLE PRINCIPALS AND OBJECTIVES

So far, we assumed that each aid project t_i has a single well-defined and measurable performance objective (B_i). This assumption can now be relaxed. Multiple and hard-to-measure performance objectives may emerge in the presence of multiple political principals, each with their own – possibly multiple – objectives. This will also force us to relax the assumption of the absence of moral hazard between political principals and their aid agencies: with multiple principals and objectives, agencies are likely to receive conflicting instructions and they cannot please everybody.

The presence of multiple political principals causes the typical problems of joint delegation, discussed in Chapter 2 in this book, and may lead to incoherent instructions to the aid agency. As a result, evaluation reports – or information feedback in general – may suit one set of principals but go against the interests of another set. The model suggests two ways to deal with this. Firstly, establish set aid projects with more vaguely defined objectives – widening the definition of B^*, and, secondly, reduce the quality of evaluation reports by widening the standard deviation on the observed B. Widening of B^* and B makes it harder to prove that an observed value/definition does not fall within a plausible range of the target value/definition. It allows the aid agency to drive an informational wedge between different and possibly conflicting interests. 'Woolly' language is the bureaucrat's trademark, for good reasons: it protects against criticism and incoherence in instructions.

European Union foreign aid programmes provide a good illustration of a situation with multiple principals and objectives. EU programmes are decided by fifteen member states that are unlikely to have identical views on the objectives of the programmes. Programme design by EC task managers is a balancing exercise between these different interests, formulating objectives in such a way that they cover all preferences without necessarily seeking coherence or unequivocally verifiable objectives. The higher the risk for divergence of interests between the agency and its political principals, the vaguer programme targets will be defined and the vaguer the quality of the evaluation reports. A consequence of such an aid agency strategy is that project definition and leverage will suffer. Those in charge of project implementation get vague and possibly even contradictory instructions; this forces them to be more careful in implementation and reduces pressure to achieve specific objectives. This illustrates how domestic policy concerns and incentive misalignment in donor – not in recipient – countries can cause poorly leveraged aid programmes.

Many external aid programmes are loan-based, for instance those run by the World Bank, the various regional development banks, the European Bank for Reconstruction and Development (EBRD) and the European Investment bank (EIB). Their lending volume does not depend on scarce fiscal revenue from member states, except in the case of subsidised loans or 'soft windows'. Funds are raised on international capital markets. This may somewhat reduce pressure from politicians since vote maximisation through political redistribution of fiscal revenue is not their concern anymore. Aid project budgets that are not financed by tax revenue are not part of politicians' objective functions (equation 5.1); consequently, political leverage on the allocation is greatly reduced. Suppliers' pressure to get a larger share of the 'market' for aid supplies may also be reduced, because they cannot claim a share of fiscal revenue here. On the other hand, loans should be repaid and lending agencies will take the necessary precautions to minimise the risk of default. Compared to grant-based aid agencies, loan-based agencies are likely to build stronger leverage and more precise performance targets into their projects because repayment may depend on performance. In line with several other authors (Frey, 1985; Rodrik, 1996) we could conclude that multilateral loan-based agencies are a better vehicle to achieve performance targets in external aid. Policy concerns of politicians, suppliers and taxpayers are somewhat more remote in the objective function of multilateral banks. However, donor country politicians may not necessarily be interested in achieving performance targets through such highly-leveraged aid agencies; they increase the risk of moral hazard between political principals and aid agencies.

6. CONCLUSIONS

The conclusions that we can draw from this analysis of the incentives and performance of foreign aid programmes are very much in line with those drawn by Downs (1957) for general government behaviour in democratic political systems: redistribution and persuasion are the politician's only tools. In the case of foreign aid programmes, political decisions on redistribution concern the amount allocated to foreign aid projects and to evaluation of these projects. Contrary to domestic transfer programmes, in foreign aid there is no direct information feedback loop between those who pay for it (taxpayers in the donor country) and those who receive the benefits (in the recipient country). This lack of direct information feedback makes foreign aid programmes particularly vulnerable to manipulation of information and facilitates the use of persuasion as a political instrument in foreign aid, especially because politicians have privileged access to project evaluation information. Only an explicit information feedback mechanism, labelled generically as 'evaluation', can correct information asymmetries in foreign aid.

However, manipulation of information feedback mechanisms often results in weak formulation of aid objectives and poorly leveraged performance incentives, thereby facilitating their derailment from the stated objectives. The presence of multiple principals worsens this situation; shifting from grants-based to loans-based aid may improve this situation. As such, performance biases in foreign aid are often the result of domestic policy concerns and incentives misalignment in donor countries, not policy misalignments in recipient countries.

Pessimism prevails with regard to the ability of evaluation to improve transparency and accountability towards taxpayers, or even to enhance aid programme performance in general; evaluation itself is subject to political manipulation. Performance variables are the outcome of political bargaining that leaves little room for manoeuvre outside the politically specified boundaries. Only factors external to the aid delivery process can bring about such structural improvements. For instance, better organised aid lobby groups may increase the external risk of discovery of poorly performing aid projects and thereby motivate aid agencies to step up the quantity and quality of evaluations in order not to be caught unaware of these problems. Changes in the political landscape, and in the preferences of the constituencies that voted a politician into office, may also affect aid programme performance.

REFERENCES

Aghion, Ph. and Tirole, J. (1997) Formal and real authority in organisations. *Journal of Political Economy*, 105(1), 1–29.

Becker, G. (1983) A theory of competition among pressure groups for political influence. *Quarterly Journal of Economics*, 63, 371–400.

DiMaggio, P. and Powell, W. (1993) The iron cage revisited: institutional isomorphism and collective rationality in the organizational fields. *American Sociological Review*, 48, 147–160.

Downs, A. (1957) *An Economic Theory of Democracy*. New York: Harper.
    (1967) *Inside Bureaucracies. Rand Corporation Research Study*. Boston, MA: Little & Brown.

Frey, B. (1985) A formulation and test of a simple model of World Bank behaviour. *Weltwirtschaftliches Archiv*, 121(3), 438–447.

Holmstrom, B. and Milgrom, P. (1991) Multitask principal–agent analysis: incentive contracts, asset ownership and job design. *Journal of Law, Economics and Organisation*, 7(s), 24–52.

Johnson, R. and Libecap, G. (1999) Information distortion and competitive remedies in government transfer programs: the case of ethanol. Paper presented at the ISNIE 1999 conference.

Rodrik, D. (1996) *Why is There Multilateral Lending?* In Proceedings of the 1995 Annual World Bank Conference on Development Economics. Washington, DC: World Bank.

Tirole, J. (1994) The internal organisation of government. *Oxford Economic Papers*, 46, 1–29.

Wittman, D. (1995) *The Myth of Democratic Failure: Why Political Institutions are Efficient*. Chicago: University of Chicago Press.

6

Some policy conclusions regarding the organisations involved in foreign aid

Bertin Martens

1. GENERAL ISSUES

The underlying theme that runs through this book is that agents involved in the delivery of foreign aid are likely to have a variety of motives and objectives that may well be very different from the publicly announced objectives of foreign aid programmes and organisations, for example, the alleviation of poverty in foreign countries. There are no doubt donors and taxpayers with genuine motives to transfer part of their wealth to alleviate poverty in foreign countries, as well as aid workers who are genuinely devoted to pursue this objective in their work and careers. However, agents involved in aid delivery may have other motives as well. Politicians in donor and recipient countries may want to use these funds to maximise their chances of being re-elected; civil servants in aid agencies and recipient organisations may seek to advance their own careers; commercial aid services contractors endeavour to maximise profits. As donors and taxpayers are not really in a position to implement these wealth transfers themselves, and potential beneficiaries are usually not in a position to mobilise the transfers on their own, delegation of tasks to agents in aid organisations is unavoidable but also carries the risk of deviation from the original objectives. This book has applied standard principal–agent theory to analyse these risks. It examines the institutional design of aid organisations and aid delivery processes and shows how different designs may favour different types of motives and thereby affect the outcomes of the delivery process. The art of institutional design is to ensure that, despite the variety of motives of agents to whom tasks were delegated, the end result remains as close as possible to the original intention of those who established the organisation.

Most of the analysis presented in this book revolved around a 'standard' model of delivery of grant-in-aid, that closely resembles the delivery channels for official bilateral aid. Voters and their political representatives in a donor country delegate the task of foreign income transfers to an official aid agency. The agency, in turn, delegates implementation tasks to private for-profit contractors who deliver the planned output to a recipient organisation, usually a government department or semi-public organisation. The recipient organisation should then ensure that the benefits reach a wider recipient country population. Several extensions and modifications of this standard model have already been pointed out. Chapter 2 discussed some aspects of the particular situation of multilateral aid agencies that are subject to the incentive problems of joint delegation. Chapter 3 discussed some issues related to project implementation by non-governmental organisations (NGOs).

Each chapter included some policy conclusions with respect to possible incentive biases and the margins for manoeuvre to improve performance at particular stages of the foreign aid delivery process. The purpose of this last chapter is not just to summarise these conclusions. Rather, we take another look at these conclusions, from the point of view of different types of aid organisations. We dig deeper into some alternative aid delivery channels and modes of implementation and investigate to what extent the policy conclusions from the 'standard' bilateral model can be applied and modified to take into account the specific circumstances and constraints that are at work in various types of aid delivery organisations such as NGOs and multilateral grant- and loan-based agencies. All these organisations have their own inherent biases, their strengths and weaknesses. Careful selection of the right organisation for various types of aid operations may exploit these inherent biases and turn them into a positive contribution to the achievement of the objectives and intentions of the donor or donor agency, and improve on aid performance compared to the 'standard' bilateral delivery mode.

The biases in the bilateral aid model are not necessarily inherent to all modes of aid delivery. Indeed, while some aid arrangements may have a negative impact on outcomes under some conditions, they may have a positive impact under other conditions. Improving aid performance then becomes a question of selecting the most appropriate delivery channel and organisation. The selection criterion proposed in this chapter revolves around alignment of objectives or motives across the aid delivery chain.

Rather than starting from the motives of donors and taxpayers, we start from the policy objectives of a bilateral donor agency. Most foreign aid is mobilised through non-voluntary taxes rather than voluntary gifts. Apart from the genuine desire to transfer wealth to the poor, a variety of other objectives may play a role in the decision to allocate foreign aid. If the ultimate objective of the donor agency is in line with the objective of its taxpaying donors, subcontractors and recipient agents, than the 'standard' way of delegation of tasks is a safe way to proceed. However, if the donor agency seeks to achieve policy objectives that may conflict with those of its intermediaries or final beneficiaries, it should try to delegate tasks to organisations that are in the best position to handle these conflicting objectives.

We start with a brief summary of the findings regarding the 'standard' official bilateral aid delivery mode and then move on to the particular characteristics of aid delivery through NGOs – non-governmental not-for-profit aid organisations. Then we look into the characteristics of multilateral aid agencies, both loan-based and grant-based types. We wind up with a discussion of the strengths and weaknesses of the aid organisation where this entire research project started: the EC. The somewhat theoretical policy conclusions of the preceding chapters will thereby be turned into more operational conclusions with regard to different types of aid organisations.

2. SPECIFIC ISSUES FOR DIFFERENT TYPES OF AID AGENCIES

Bilateral agencies

The studies in this book have demonstrated that at least part of the responsibility for the performance of foreign aid lies with aid suppliers and their intermediaries, rather than with recipients.

Incentive biases in the various steps and organisations involved in the aid delivery process may explain some of the structural biases in outcomes. Some of these biases are inherent to public agencies in general while others can be attributed to the nature of foreign aid in particular. Within the 'standard' official bilateral aid delivery model, two types of biases have been identified.

Firstly, official aid agencies are public agencies and, as such, subject to the typical incentive problems that are common to all public agencies: multiple principals and objectives. Official aid agencies are accountable to a variety of political principals who represent different interests and therefore emphasise different aspects and objectives for the programmes run by the agency. They are accountable to parliamentarians who represent all kinds of political and commercial interests; they have to respond to a variety of domestic interest groups and their lobbying representatives. The wider the range of political principals and interest groups to which the agency has to respond, the vaguer the agency's mission and the weaker the performance incentives. Agencies that have to combine the concerns of export lobbies, commercial aid services suppliers, charitable organisations and environmental groups into a single project are often forced to broaden and weaken, and even blur, the formulation of project objectives. Since objectives of foreign aid projects are anyway often hard to measure or verify, further broadening makes it even more difficult to calculate trade-offs between the, often inconsistent, objectives of political principals and interest groups.

Secondly, official aid agencies suffer from a typical problem that is characteristic of foreign aid: a broken feedback loop. Contrary to domestic aid programmes, the assumed beneficiaries of foreign aid have no political leverage on the sponsors and decision-makers in the donor country. Sponsors and beneficiaries live in different constituencies; beneficiaries have no voting rights or other political channels through which they can voice their concerns and influence decision-making. Consequently, foreign aid decision-making is usually a function of preferences of donor-country interest groups, not the preferences of recipient countries and beneficiaries. As a result, beneficiaries may sometimes receive aid packages that include objectives and conditions that they would prefer not to receive. This is where divergent objectives in the aid delivery process start to emerge.

These two types of incentive biases in foreign aid agencies generate several biased outcomes that can be frequently observed in aid delivery processes:

- Inputs and procedural bias, vaguely specified policies and programmes, and weak performance incentives in official aid agencies.
- Substantial discretion for subcontractors that may facilitate both collusion and conflict with recipient organizations, depending on the terms of the subcontract.
- Project outcomes that are poorly embedded in the social, political and economic tissue of the recipient country.
- Vaguely specified and hard-to-verify project outcomes, that undermine the usefulness and leverage of evaluations.

These biases are inherent in the 'standard' set-up of official bilateral aid delivery processes and are there to stay. They cannot be completely neutralised without eliminating the organisations in which they are embedded. What can be done however is to modify some aspects of the institutional set-up so as to reduce the extent of these biases.

The extent of multiple political principals and objectives in official bilateral aid is affected, for instance, by the internal coherence of a coalition government. If coalitions include a wide range of parties and views, policy programmes are likely to be broader and more vaguely defined. On the other hand, agencies could exploit differences in preferences among political principals, play them off against each other and forge coalitions in support of particular projects. Unbundling of this variety of objectives into individual and well-defined projects could also enhance project focus and performance. For instance, aid budgets could be allocated to different policy objectives, each with their own budget line. The overall allocation would have to satisfy a political balance, but within each budget line political factions could impose their own more coherent set of views.

The political constituency of the minister responsible for foreign aid will also have an impact on aid programme specifications and evaluations, thereby affecting likely outcomes. Ministers whose constituency is based among commercial aid services suppliers are likely to chose different programme specifications and evaluation parameters than ministers who are strongly linked to groups that favour genuine wealth transfers to beneficiary countries.

Agencies will inevitably suffer from a degree of excessive focus upon routine procedural activities and project inputs management tasks, such as financial and contract procedures and tendering of supplies. Projects will tend to be selected for ease of monitoring and speed of disbursement, rather than overall contribution to beneficiary welfare. Well-known biases in aid programmes towards large infrastructure projects and quick-disbursing budgetary support programmes are good examples. Personnel recruitment and promotion will rely upon performance in routine procedural tasks, even for staff that should carry out tasks that require more substantive judgment. As a result, staff with more substantive knowledge on development aid issues will tend to have poorer career prospects. These biases can be reduced to some extent by unbundling of tasks that require different skill sets. For instance, separation of financial and contractual management tasks from substantive policy formulation and analysis tasks would allow agents to demonstrate their skills in each of these domains, and promotions could take account of these differences in skills.

The contractual set-up as well as the type of contractor affects the likelihood of discretionary and collusive behavior. Whether the contractor is an NGO or a profit-seeking consultant can change the effectiveness of project implementation. NGOs may push harder to achieve their goals, even at the cost of foregoing some or all of the profits on a contract. Profit-seeking consultants may more easily be drawn into collusive behavior with the recipient, if the latter holds control over payments. However, if the donor holds control over payments, the reverse may be true. Also, the history of previous relationships between the contractor, the recipient and the donor matters, because it will affect the possibility that a bargaining outcome is reached. If efficiency is the goal and bargaining should be discouraged, than contractors who are unfamiliar with a country should be given control of the project.

The optimal configuration of project implementation arrangements depends critically on whether embeddedness or interest group influence is particularly important in the project being implemented. Bilateral donor agencies may actually seek to use aid in such a way as to promote the interests of specific groups, both in their domestic constituency and in the recipient country. For instance, they may seek to promote the foreign business interest of domestic aid services suppliers' companies through tied aid contracts and restricted tenders, terms of reference with fuzzy specifications, procedural rather than substantive control on project implementation and the absence of evaluations. Bilateral aid may also seek to promote specific interests in the recipient country that are aligned with its own interests. For instance, groups that promote political and economic ties to the (often ex-colonial power) donor country or groups that seek institutional and policy reforms that are in line with donor preferences but not necessarily widely accepted in the recipient country.

In both cases, bilateral aid arrangements can be modulated accordingly. Control over project implementation can be delegated to the domestic or recipient country interest group whose preferences are in line with the policy objectives of the aid agency. This saves on monitoring and evaluation costs for the aid agency. If control is handed over to an interest group in the recipient country, it may also solve problems related to the embeddedness of reforms, provided that the interest group itself is sufficiently widely embedded in recipient country society. Typically, however, many groups claim to support the donor's goals; in that case there is an incentive compatibility problem. If the interest group represents narrow interests only, a collective action problem may arise, thereby lowering rather than improving the chances of successful reform. In the latter case, a bilateral aid channel may not be appropriate, for two reasons. Firstly, the donor may have to overcome substantial resistance in the recipient country, which may not come without political costs for both donor and recipient governments. Secondly, donor leverage on reforms is likely to increase if donors exercise collective pressure. To diminish the risks of political fall-out costs and increase the chances of successful action, bilateral donors may wish to channel their resources through multilateral agencies rather than interest groups with whom they have close political affiliations.

Non-Governmental Organisations (NGOs)

NGOs exist in many varieties. They may be single-issue organizations – 'save the whale' – or seek to promote a wider policy domain such as environmental concerns, democracy, human rights or religious causes. NGOs may have thousands of members but they usually hold a fairly similar set of preferences regarding the issue that the NGO intends to promote. This greatly reduces multiple principals and objectives problems in NGO management. The narrower the NGOs objective is formulated and the more homogenous the preference set of its members, the more focused their actions can be. Inconsistencies and trade-off's between various actions are less likely to occur.

Furthermore, to the extent that NGOs are able to find and collaborate with like-minded recipient groups in beneficiary countries, preferences of donors and recipients will be aligned and conflicts of interest can be avoided. The end result will be collusive behaviour between the donor country NGO, both as a donor and as a contractor, and the recipient country organisation, both furthering the objectives of the project on which they hold identical or a least very similar ideas. There is less need for monitoring of project outcomes since the objectives of sponsors, contractors and recipients are convergent. This also helps to close the broken feedback loop, a very typical problem of official foreign aid. Because of convergent preferences, the recipient's comments on actions and outcomes is much more likely to be taken into account by the implementing donor country NGO. Recipient feedback does affect donor decision-making in this case. Finally, if the recipient country NGO is well-embedded in the target community for the aid project, than embeddedness-related implementation problems, discussed in chapter 4, may also be avoided.

'Twinning' projects are a good example of this type of NGO-based co-operation: aid is delivered by 'twinning' of like-minded organisations in donor and recipient countries. For instance, an accountants' association in the donor country is 'twinned' with a similar association in the recipient country to define and implement accounting standards and train accountants to apply them. Other examples include 'twinning' of a wide range of professional organisations, but also commercial organisations like banks and public institutions like local governments and community service organisations. Similarity in the objectives of twinning partners ensures strong collusive behavior to achieve the intended project outcome.

Delegation of aid programme implementation to NGOs may have several advantages for official aid agencies. First, aid agencies that seek to avoid the problems of multiple objectives and the related inconsistencies and trade-off problems, can unbundle these objectives and select issue-specific NGOs to implement them as separate contracts. Once a budgetary deal is reached and a budget line for each objective is agreed, the role of the aid agency is limited to signing a contract with the subcontracting NGOs. That way, the implementation of possibly contentious projects is split across a variety of organisations and possible inconsistencies and trade-off problems are avoided. There is little need for monitoring by the official aid agency. The NGOs can be expected to pursue the issues vigorously, even beyond their profit constraint, because the preferences of their members are in line with the project objectives. Aid agency control is limited to verification of financial and administrative procedures, not substantive implementation issues.

A domain that is well suited for NGO involvement is humanitarian aid, including food and medical aid to populations in urgent need. Humanitarian aid usually generates very widespread political support in both donor and recipient countries. In terms of the models presented in this book, there is a strong overlap in objectives between donors, implementing agents and recipients in the case of humanitarian aid: all agents in the aid delivery chain agree that alleviation of the needs of the affected population is the single overriding concern. Collusive behaviour between the agents involved in aid delivery and implementation should be encouraged in these circumstances. Implementation through for-profit private companies, rather than NGOs, would introduce a different objective (profit) that might interrupt this strong alignment of preferences in the delivery chain and could even be perceived as unethical. Involvement of government bureaucracies that have their own internal procedural logic may also be perceived as inappropriate in these cases. Fast and up-front delegation of tasks from bilateral aid agencies to humanitarian NGOs avoids these problems.

On the other hand, narrow-focused NGOs are often lacking wider political embeddedness in donor and recipient country societies and may thereby trigger political reactions. NGOs and twinning partners may vigorously pursue narrow objectives that are not widely appreciated, either in the donor or in the recipient country. For instance, humanitarian NGOs can get involved in collusive behaviour with the perpetrators of humanitarian emergencies, in order to achieve their objectives without taking into account the wider consequences of such behaviour. Their narrowness of focus is sometimes a big handicap, for instance when they focus entirely on the losers from a project and don't look at the benefits the project creates. They are no less liable than other aid organisations to superficial focus on more easily observable variables, such as food and medicines delivered, at the expense of more lasting but hard-to-measure development goals.

To the extent that their activities are financed with private contributions and channelled to private recipients, donor and recipient governments may avoid getting caught up in these issues. However, to the extent that they are publicly financed, some degree of political control over their activities and policies will be required. Many bilateral donor agencies have solved these problems by financing NGOs that are embedded in wider socio-political networks in their home country. For instance, they channel aid through NGOs affiliated with political parties, labour unions, religious groups and other well-established social organisations. These affiliations reduce an NGOs margin for discretionary behaviour and give the donor agency and government a variety of means to exercise political pressure to reign in inappropriate behaviour, if need be.

Also, the fact that most NGOs are financially dependent on contracts with the aid agency enables the agency to exercise some degree of control over NGO behaviour. NGOs may actually become bureaucracies in their own right and thereby divert their agents' behavioural motives towards financial and career concerns.

In conclusion, NGOs can help official bilateral aid agencies to reduce some of the problems related to multiple objectives. Delegation of aid implementation tasks to NGOs can be beneficial in cases of strong convergence of objectives between the NGO and the final recipients, or at least between the aid agency and the NGO. However, care should be taken to avoid too strong collusive behaviour between the NGO and the interest groups that it serves, which may create political problems.

Multilateral agencies

As explained in Chapter 2, multilateral aid agencies are cases of joint delegation: many member states delegate the implementation of aid programmes to a single organisation. This may exacerbate the typical problems of multiple and conflicting objectives that we found in bilateral aid agencies and have a negative effect on the organisation's performance. On the other hand, multilateral organisations may be in a better position to play off members against each other, form coalitions, induce collective action among members and, in general, achieve objectives that individual members would not be able to achieve on their own. As pointed out in chapter 2, multilateral aid agencies can justify their existence if their unique achievements outweigh the negative impact of joint delegation problems. The question then is: what could these unique achievements be?

The answer to this question depends to a large extent on the type of multilateral aid agency. Two categories can be identified. Firstly, multilateral development banks (MDBs) that operate on the basis of loans, mobilised on international capital markets. Examples include the World Bank and the regional development banks like the European Bank for Reconstruction and Development (EBRB) and the African, Asian and Interamerican Development Banks, amongst others. Secondly, multilateral aid agencies that operate through grants, financed with fiscal revenue from donor countries: the United Nations Development Programme, the United Nations High Commissioner for Refugees (UNHCR) and various other United Nations agencies involved in development programmes, and also the aid programmes of the European Commission (EC).

These very different financing modalities[1] have an impact on a multilateral agency's margins for discretionary decision-making and exploitation of the advantages of joint delegation situations. To the extent that a multilateral agency uses fiscal revenue, transferred by an official national aid agency, there is still a strong interest by the donor country and bilateral agency in the use of these funds. After all, national taxpayers, their political representatives and interest groups will want to know how taxpayers' money is being used and would want to use it to further their own national interests and objectives. When multilateral agencies have their own sources of funds, however, mobilised on international capital markets, national political interest wanes; there is no taxpayers' money involved anymore. This gives the management of the multilateral donor agency more room for discretionary decision making, independent of national interests.

Weakening the political link between donors and financial resources, combined with majority voting in the Board, enables MDBs to play off members against each other, forge coalitions and, in general, induce collective action that would be hard for individual donors to undertake on their own. It also weakens the link between donors' and MDBs' objectives and strengthens the position of the bank with regard to the borrower country.

Unpopular policy measures and conditionality can be more easily imposed on the borrower. Donors will feel less politically responsible for these unpopular measures and recipients find it more difficult to put pressure on a wide range of more remotely involved donors than on a single directly involved bilateral donor. In short, aid is best channelled through MDBs when there is strong divergence or even conflict between donors' and recipients' objectives, when donors want to impose unpopular conditionality on aid resources and prefer not to be too closely associated with that conditionality.

MDBs do not only offer attractive institutional solutions for donor countries; they also have strong attraction for recipient countries, despite the conditionalities that are often attached to their resources. To understand this, it is necessary to explain their financial

---

[1] Most multilateral development banks also have so-called 'soft windows' whereby grant financing is mixed with loans in order to subsidise interest rates below market rates. This mixes the characteristics of both types of multilateral organisations.

mechanisms, in particular the way they handle portfolio risks (guarantees) and the pricing of these risks (interest rates). MDBs are established by member states that contribute a fixed amount of capital. Only a small part of that capital is actually paid in; the remainder is 'callable' in case the MDB incurs losses that need to be covered by its members. This constitutes a guarantee fund to cover any potential losses and against which the MDB can borrow on international capital markets, up to a fixed 'gearing' ratio. As that borrowing is mostly guaranteed by member states with the highest credit ratings, the cost of borrowing for MDBs is very low. They pass on this interest rate benefit to borrowing countries. On top of the guarantee provided by callable capital, all lending is covered by a sovereign guarantee from the borrower government. This guarantee may not be worth much on international financial markets where the borrower's credit rating is usually very low. But combined with the MDBs preferred creditor status it forces borrowers to keep on serving multilateral debt until the very limit of their financial means.[2] Furthermore, most MDBs operate as 'co-operative clubs': both borrowers and lenders are members and shareholders in the bank. All members have the right to borrow at the same interest rate, irrespective of country or specific project risk. Loan pricing is generally not modulated in function of portfolio risks.

There exist of course many variations on this basic theme. For example, the London-based European Bank for Reconstruction and Development (EBRD) has channelled a majority of its loans to private sector borrowers in the transition economies of Eastern Europe and the former Soviet Union and dropped the usual guarantee mechanisms; they are not covered by recipient state guarantees or preferred creditor status. Any losses are to be covered by the EBRD's internal reserves only, as happened in the aftermath of the Russian crisis in 1998. This provides an incentive for the EBRD to make better decisions, for each project: if the loan does not perform, there is no guarantee from the recipient country government to cover it up. Another example is the Luxemburg-based European Investment Bank (EIB). Rather than doing away with the

---

[2] This implies that, if multilateral debt is not serviced, all other types of official lending are stopped. It also includes immunity from Paris Club debt rescheduling in case debt is not serviced.

usual guarantees, it has increased them. EIB lending to countries outside the EU benefits from a triple guarantee: callable capital from EU member states, the sovereign guarantee of the borrowing country government and a guarantee from the EC budget. Consequently, specific project risks have become virtually irrelevant in EIB credit decisions.

From a neo-classical competitive markets' point of view, the financial arrangements of MDBs represent obvious incentives misalignments that falsify competition and distort pricing in financial markets; they should be abolished. What keeps them in place? Clearly, these financial arrangements are favourable to borrowing countries. They get a financial advantage, at the cost of policy conditionalities. Firstly, MDBs offer loans at rates far below the international financial market rates that developing countries would normally have to pay – if they have market access at all. Borrowers cannot find a better deal on financial markets, which gives the MDBs considerable leverage over loan conditions and conditionalities. Secondly, MDBs offer the same interest rates to all their members, irrespective of sovereign country risks and project risks, and without discrimination.[3] By treating all borrowers on an equal footing, it gives them no reason to form coalitions against the MDB.

But MDBs also have their build-in weaknesses. Firstly, they are banks. Although they are not profit maximisers, they should avoid losses and ensure an adequate financial performance of their credit portfolio. This may affect their stance on policy conditionality and induce collusive behavior with their debtors, so as to ensure a continued debt service. Many studies have shown the potential for moral hazard and ineffectiveness of the conditionality of MDBs. Secondly, the ability of the MDBs to keep donor countries at arms' length and play them off against each other under majority voting, depends on the weight of a donor in the vote count. As donor's votes are correlated with their share in the capital of the MDBs, a single large shareholder – such as the US – may still lean heavily

---

[3] Even MDBs that are not co-operative clubs (i.e. borrowers are not members of the club), such as the EIB and the Islamic Development Bank, still use a single across-the-board interest rate. Except for the 'soft windows', such as the World Bank's International Development Association-window, which are usually reserved for the poorest countries.

on policy decisions. The policy of MDBs may then run the risk of becoming a tool of that shareholder's foreign policy objectives.

In short, MDBs have managed to circumvent some of the problems and exploit the advantage associated with joint delegation. They offer donor countries a politically less contentious channel for collective action and, at the same time, provide borrowing developing countries with substantial financial advantages. On top of this, they manage to marry the, often conflicting, objectives of donor and recipient countries, at a price to both: the relative independence of MDBs. The attractiveness of this channel for development aid, for all parties concerned, may explain their success.

The European Commission as multilateral aid agency

This leaves us with the second category of grant-based multilateral aid agencies, such as the United Nations Development Programme (UNDP) and other UN agencies, and the EC – the agency that provided the starting point for this entire research project.

Grant-based multilateral agencies have a major disadvantage compared to MDBs: They use taxpayers' money from donor countries, which makes it harder to keep donors' national political and economic interests at arm's length. Obviously, donor representatives will want to keep a close eye on how that money is spent and further their own interests through that spending process. UN agencies operate as co-operative clubs, with both donors and beneficiary countries represented in decision-making. The presence of beneficiaries may somewhat water down the influence of the donors but may also generate donor frustration. The EC's institutional set-up differs in two crucial respects from the UNs: beneficiary countries are not involved in decision-making and most relevant decisions are taken by unanimity, not by majority, in the EC Council. These make it harder for the EC as a multilateral aid organisation to circumvent the disadvantages and exploit the advantages of joint delegation.

The studies in this book have pointed out two basic institutional factors that have contributed to persistent biases in the EC's multilateral foreign aid programs: multiple political principals and multiple objectives. National ministers in charge of a bilateral donor agency can take political ownership of their development policies and strategies. The minister defends them in parliament where a coalition or political majority reduces the number of political principals and interests from many to a few or, ideally, just one. By contrast, an EC commissioner in charge of foreign aid has to deal with fifteen member states and hundreds of European parliamentarians, without a political coalition to support the proposed policies in the Council or in the European Parliament. Consequently, EC foreign aid policy formulation tends to be broader, vaguer and less well-defined, taking into account the views and opinions of a wide range of parties. This makes implementation more difficult and less efficient and obfuscates performance evaluation efforts. The absence of majority voting for most decisions in the Council does not facilitate matters, on the contrary.

While the usual biased incentives that lead to inputs bias in bilateral aid agencies are also present in EC aid, they are amplified by strong competition between member states to increase their share in the contracts cake. Member states support their own private aid services suppliers in this competition. National aid service suppliers actively lobby their political representatives in Brussels for that purpose; national representatives in EC foreign aid decision-making committees spend a considerable part of their time exploring and pursuing contract opportunities for national suppliers. This focuses attention very much on inputs and procurement procedures (budgets, contracts, tenders, etc.), thereby further tilting the bias in favour of inputs and away from outputs and performance. There is more potential political dynamite in a failure to follow the correct procedures for tenders, contracts and expenditures than in a failure to achieve overall project objectives, despite the fact that the latter situation may turn the entire project expenditure into a waste. Because of the absence of political ownership at EC level and intensive competition between member states, inputs bias in EC aid is likely to be stronger than in bilateral aid programmes.

On the other hand, the EC is not in a good position to exploit the advantages of joint delegation from its member states to a multilateral aid organisation. Firstly, it is not a bank but a grant-dispensing agency. It uses tax money and that prevents it from keeping member states' political and economic interests at arm's length. At the same time, this prevents the EC from putting strong conditionality on its aid programmes, trying to achieve reforms that member states find hard to do on their own. The close involvement of member states in decision-making could induce a political backlash to such programmes. The EC is not in a good position to drive a wedge between member states and beneficiary countries interests by juggling with conditionality and financial conditions, like MDBs do.

Secondly, it is not in a good position to promote collective action among EU member states in the use of its foreign aid. A large part of EU foreign aid is still channelled through the member states' bilateral aid channels and organisations. Despite years of attempts at aid co-ordination, member states still go their own way in most aid decisions.

Thirdly, the EC as a multilateral aid organisation is not a co-operative club of donors and beneficiaries. Beneficiary countries do not participate in decision-making and are not in a position to water down the exclusive pursuit of donor-country interests.[4]

Fourthly, the EC is not in a good position to play off member states against each other and form coalitions around particular development programmes and themes. Most relevant decision-making in the Council follows the unanimity rule; one dissenting member state is sufficient to block a decision. There is no reason for member states to form coalitions or join forces with the Commission to force a breakthrough.

This research has shown that the EC's predicament is by no means exceptional in the world of foreign aid, that it is due to institutional incentives structures and that there are ways to improve this performance or at least mitigate some of the consequences of the biased performance incentives that underlay the institutional set-up of the EC's foreign aid programmes. Ideally, the number of political principals overseeing EC foreign aid could be reduced to one if EC proposals were supported by a political majority coalition in Parliament and/or if majority voting in the Council were introduced for matters pertaining to foreign aid. However, this will require more fundamental EU institutional reforms that go far

---

[4] Except for the prerogatives of the Joint EU–African, Caribbean and Pacific Parliamentary Assembly under the Lome Convention, where parliamentarians of both donor and beneficiary countries have a seat and a vote.

beyond the domain of foreign aid only. As a second-best solution, the recent creation of a specialised EC foreign aid agency – Europe Aid – may be a step in the right direction, provided that it gets clear mission orders, reducing the number of objectives, stating them more clearly and limiting interference by multiple principals. Some degree of political independence for this aid agency could be achieved through changes in procedures, such as majority voting on aid programmes and budgets. Finally, enhanced monitoring and evaluation of aid programme outcomes could help to strengthen the information feedback loop between beneficiaries and donors/taxpayers. But it is unlikely to be effective unless fully independent from political principals who manage aid programmes. Last but not least, one can conclude from this research that the usual suspect for poor performance of EC aid – the presumed lack of human resources – is unlikely to be the real culprit. Human resources are bogged down in unproductive and inefficient administrative procedures and inputs-related approaches, drawing them away from more results-oriented tasks. Increasing the number of staff without fundamental changes in the incentives structures would only worsen input bias because it would create opportunities to pile up more ineffective layers of procedures. The only real solution is a fundamental reform of the incentives that staff are confronted with.

Index